Everybody Wins, Except for Most of Us
What Economics Teaches About Globalization

BY JOSH BIVENS

Economic
Policy
Institute

Table of Contents

ACKNOWLEDGMENTS

It's surprising that completing even a project as modest as this incurs so many debts, but, it has, and acknowledgment must be made.

Several colleagues offered advice or support along the way. Chief among them was John Schmitt, who ploughed through the technical chapters and offered as many searching questions as points of encouragement—both were hugely useful. Robert Lynch, Larry Mishel, Rob Scott, and John Irons all read portions of the manuscript and offered useful insights and suggestions.

If the book reads well at all, it's due to the efforts of Pat Watson, who also provided the title. I personally think it's the best part of the book.

Obviously, any good in this book is over-determined by the efforts of the generous people above. The abundant bad in it is my failure to appreciate their attempts to steer me somewhere more useful.

Funding for the book came from the Sloan Foundation, and their support, especially that of Gail Pesyna, is hugely appreciated.

Lastly, and most important, while Holley and Finn were probably bad for the book (making work look bad relative to just hanging lazily out at home), they do make working, and everything else, a lot more worthwhile.

Executive Summary

A wide gulf exists today in American politics. On one side are voters anxious about globalization and its impact on their ability to make a good living. On the other are economists, policy makers, and pundits who maintain that trade is good for the economy and that the only problem it raises is that its large benefits are too broadly diffused throughout the population for any single voter to notice.

And so these policy makers and opinion leaders have taken it upon themselves to educate the American public about the benefits of the globalization status quo, resting their effort heavily on the suggestion that "all economists believe" globalization is good for American workers.

The problem for this approach is that those worried about what the integration of a rich U.S. economy and a much poorer global economy means for their living standards have a better grasp of the underlying economics. Open the international trade textbook and one will find two key predictions about this global integration: it can indeed harm the majority of American workers, and it actually does have a natural constituency—the most economically privileged Americans. Not for nothing is economics called the dismal science.

Given these textbook predictions, it should come as no surprise that the two starkest economic developments of the past 30 years—rising inequality and the increasing integration of the United States into a poorer global economy—are causally connected. The debate among researchers who have delved into this topic is generally not a disagreement about the predicted *direction* of trade's influence but rather an empirical argument about the size of its contribution to the historic run-up in inequality seen over the past several decades. Some economists think trade explains a major portion of the rise in inequality; others believe that it explains very little. A large majority pegs the contribution somewhere between 10% and 40% of the total rise in inequality in the 1980s and early 1990s. This book shows that its influence has only become stronger since.

To date, the redistributive effect of trade has largely been a response to global integration of the manufacturing sector. The impact of the rise of trade in services, a sector once thought to be largely insulated from global competition, is starting to come into focus. Offshoring of service work potentially gives globalization a much larger lever with which to affect domestic labor market outcomes, and it could have huge implications for the future shape of earnings for American workers.

A key contribution of this book is simply to translate the costs of globalization for workers on the losing end into easily understandable terms: dollars per worker (or household). Using the best practices identified in the earlier trade and wages debate, this book finds that the annual losses to a full-time median-wage earner in 2006 total approximately $1,400. For a typical household with two earners, the loss is more than $2,500. These losses are as high or higher than other economic costs commonly presented as much more damaging to American families, such as the cost of health care, spikes in gasoline and fuel oil prices, the cost of a child's four-year college education, or the funds needed to remedy a possible shortfall in the future of Social Security.

To deal with a harm as large and widespread as that imposed by globalization, we need to think much more ambitiously about public policy that re-links aggregate and individual prosperity, a policy that uses all the levers available: social insurance, public investment, fairer economic rules, and redistribution when other tools fail to provide egalitarian outcomes. Further, despite much protestation to the contrary, the globalization *status quo* is at least as stingy to the poor trading partners of the United States as it is to American workers. There is no real danger to progressive goals in calling for its complete upending.

So far we have been content to allow globalization without compensation to proceed apace. This complacency has already hurt us, and the damage will only grow in the future.

Globalization and the new economic insecurity

It was 1995, in the middle of Bill Clinton's first administration, and Robert Rubin, his new Treasury secretary, was pondering the lessons of his first big political fight. The Mexican government had been on the brink of default, but initial strong support in Congress for his rescue effort had deteriorated day by day. In the end he had had to put aside congressional approval and act on his own by tapping $20 billion in discretionary Treasury Department funds. In the future, he concluded, the key to political support would be public support:

> At some point during the second term, Secretary of State Madeleine Albright and I discussed holding joint public meetings around the country to try to improve how public understanding of global issues...affect people's lives. Regrettably we never did this, but some kind of ongoing public education campaign is badly needed to change the politics around all these concerns.... On trade, for example, dislocations are very specific and keenly felt—and lead to strong political action—but the benefits of both exports and imports are widely dispersed and not recognized as trade-related, and thus haven't developed the level of political support they require. (Rubin and Weisberg 2003, 37-38)

It is regrettable that Secretary Rubin never mounted his public education campaign, but not because American workers, from waitresses and office assistants and auto workers to software engineers, lawyers, and stock brokers, were deprived of an economics lesson. It is regrettable because he may have missed a chance to learn that the misinformed people in need of enlightening actually understand textbook trade economics just fine.

Take one particularly prominent skeptic of the idea that globalization must be good for all American workers:

> Last December...I was being driven to the Stockholm airport. Along the road we passed many of Sweden's best factories. They seemed to the tourist's eye to have lost some of their bright glitter and busy-ness....Now there is nothing that these factories can do which cannot be done almost as well in the Pacific Basin—and often with Asian labor at real wage rates only half that prevailing in Sweden. And surely much the same can be said about factories in

Turin, Brussels, Birmingham, and Chicago....Of course, the most resourceful Swedish and American operations can survive at some positive level. But all of us cannot be above average. As the billions of people who live in East Asia and Latin America qualify for good, modern jobs, the half billion European and North Americans who used to tower over the rest of the world will find their upward progress in living standards encountering tough resistance. (Bhagwati and Dehejia 1994)

This particular skeptic, however, probably wouldn't benefit much from an educational campaign: he's already won a Nobel Prize and essentially founded the modern discipline of economics. Paul Samuelson wrote these words after attending a Nobel jubilee in 1992, and they are a good summary of the textbook predictions of what happens to most workers living in a rich country when its economy integrates with a much poorer global economy.

While this integration generally makes both countries a bit richer, it has much more powerful effects on the distribution of income *within* each economy. For the United States, this redistribution swamps the efficiency gains for most workers, making them worse off not just compared to globalization's winners, but in *absolute* terms.

Secretary Rubin's focus on the *national* advantages of trade over its contribution to economic inequality is hardly unique. It's almost impossible to find a mainstream politician or policy maker, or newspaper editorial board or reporter or TV commentator—of any ideological stripe—who doesn't aver that trade is an all-around good thing; "win-win" is the most common formulation. But if you raise the point that trade redistributes income and creates some winners but many losers, a point predicted by standard economic theory and proven in empirical studies—you're made to feel somewhat unseemly, that you and those people you're concerned about should have stayed in school longer or have studied something different or just been smarter. In other words, when trade makes software engineers richer, that's economics. When it makes Americans without a four-year college degree (the large majority of workers) poorer, that's their own failure to adapt to the New Economy. And when trade agreements prohibit a country from copying the technology it buys, that's good business. But if agreements required that each country protect the most basic rights afforded to its workers, that would be protectionism.

The economics of international trade are actually quite straightforward, and the first aim of this book is to introduce readers to the economic theory and studies that show us clearly that the trade story is not win-win but rather good news-bad news: good news for national incomes, bad news for many if not most individuals and families, because their income is redistributed away from them and up the income ladder. The big unanswered question regarding globalization is what to do about the winners and losers—who gets what, when, how, and whether. That is, we need a real *political* debate about globalization.

Globalization's place in modern American politics was secured in the furious debate over the North American Free Trade Agreement (NAFTA) in 1993. More recently, the growing gap between the very rich and the rest and the fragility of middle-class living standards have become part of the political conversation as well. Although inequality and insecurity are not all that new—numerous academic studies have demonstrated forcefully that they have been rising for roughly 30 years—what is new is their elevation as issues of prime political importance.

Help wanted: straighter talk on globalization

While economic theory argues that global integration leads to lower wages for the majority of American workers, at each stage in the trade debate policy makers, opinion leaders, and even progressive economists have often minimized these costs of globalization. Instead of, say, trying to inform the public that the real action of globalization in affecting U.S. workers is slower wage growth, not fewer jobs in the economy, they have chosen instead to say simply that "trade doesn't affect jobs" and then let the silence afterward imply that fears about globalization are groundless. Why this group would misrepresent the true implications of globalization for American living standards is a tough question (the sociology of the economics profession and just flat ignorance on the part of many about the economics of international trade both surely play a role). But *how* these misrepresentations are expressed is easier to pinpoint. Watch for them.

The first *how* is conflating national *income* and national *welfare*. As global integration generally raises national income (gross domestic product, or GDP), many economists rest arguments for it there. If pressed, they often argue that concern about how this national income is distributed post-integration is just not their business—that's politics, not economics. This is a dodge, pure and simple. Economists expressing a preference for global integration are, in fact, expressing a *purely* political or ethical preference, not a scientific judgment. Nothing in the discipline of economics tells us that a policy that raises national income but leaves some individuals better off and some worse off is one that raises national welfare.

The only criterion by which economists can make firm, *value-free* judgments about economic policies and trends is what is called the *Pareto principle*. Pareto optimality results only when an economic change makes one person better off *without harming anybody else*. Clearly, the outcomes of globalization in the U.S. economy are not Pareto optimal.

A weaker criterion sometimes put forward by economists is *compensated* Pareto improvement. This criterion argues that if the outcome of an economic policy or trend even makes it *possible* to make everybody better off, then it should be embraced. Given that there are net national gains from global integration, compensated Pareto improvement says that they must be grabbed. But this is absolutely a judgment rooted in politics and values, not just economic logic. Unless one is willing to argue that taking a dollar from an apparel worker to give a dollar and change to Donald

Trump is good for America, we can make no inference about the impact of global integration on national welfare until compensation for its costs *actually happens.*

In any case, compensated Pareto improvement as a guide to assessing economic policy is routinely violated. If professional economists were polled as to whether the Bush tax cuts should be financed with across-the-board cuts in government spending, a majority (or at least a strong plurality) would probably say no. Yet, judged from strict compensated Pareto improvement, this policy could be a clear winner: tax cuts financed by spending cuts should (trivially) boost overall national income. It's time the profession started asking itself more seriously why compensated Pareto improvement applies so forcefully only to globalization.

Another key strategy for minimizing the costs of globalization is to scale them against inappropriate benchmarks. The most common comparison weighs the upward redistribution caused by globalization against the *total* redistribution that has occurred in recent decades. The problem with this comparison is that this overall rise in inequality has been so huge that even a non-majority part of it translates into thousands of dollars of losses for workers on the losing end, losses which repeat (and grow, as trade flows grow), year after year. Globalization might be a minority player behind the rise in inequality, but it's not a minor one.

Lastly, there is a common distortion of the globalization debate in the United States that is rooted, at least, in a sound progressive concern: access to the U.S. market creates opportunity for the world's poorest workers and must be safeguarded on these grounds. The concern is real and ethical, but it is not necessarily one well-served by obfuscation regarding globalization's impact on American workers. Further, it's a concern not at all well-served by the globalization status quo. While those expressing angst about globalization are frequently tarred as protectionists who want to choke off access to the U.S. market for exports from poor nations, the truth is that the globalization *status quo* provides this access only at a heavy price. This price is generally a radical reduction in the policy-making autonomy of U.S. trading partners, a reduction demanded in the treaties routinely mislabeled "free trade agreements." These agreements generally make liberal access to the U.S. market contingent upon the adoption of a range of policies that are not necessarily trade-related but that *are* amenable to the global corporate class. Today's warriors for the globalization status quo have little reason to preen about what they've delivered to the poor nations of the world, and progressives shouldn't be at all queasy about calling for a fundamental re-thinking of the global trading system.

Compensation: How much, and how delivered?

There is an enormous chasm between the income losses felt by American workers on the wrong end of global integration and the solutions that are generally prescribed to compensate them for their troubles. Ironically, even those advocating for workers harmed by globalization often end up demanding weaker medicine than the economics warrant.

An utterly appropriate demand in trade policy is that all trade agreements establish the adoption and enforcement of labor standards protecting workers' rights as a precondition to favorable access to the U.S. consumer market. This is good economics and good politics, for a number of reasons. What it is not, however, is particularly protective of American living standards in the face of global integration.

Another appropriate reform of globalization as currently practiced concerns the utterly non-trade-related clutter (generally originating in demands from the corporate sector) that finds its way into almost all trade agreements, including agreements for membership in the World Trade Organization. Commitments to enforce U.S.-style intellectual property laws, the restructuring of financial sector regulations, and detailed protections of investor rights against expropriation (defined liberally at times to include any government policy that hurts profits) constitute the lion's share of these agreements. Many advocates insist that the overweighing of corporate interests over all others has resulted in trade agreements that harm U.S. workers by straying too far from simple and clean trade liberalization. They also rightfully point out the irony: if you want free trade, why do you need all these agreements and protections?

Like the push for worker protections, the campaign against corporate clutter in trade agreements is good economics and good politics, but not particularly protective of American living standards in the immediate future. The first-order threat to the living standards of U.S. workers posed by integration of the United States and global economies stems from the very fact of this integration, not its terms. The terms of integration can lead to marginal improvements in outcomes for American workers (maybe more substantial improvements over a long time horizon). More important, these terms have great influence on the effect of global integration on less-developed countries. For these reasons, it is vital to get these terms right. Even when we do, however, the very fact that a comparatively rich and labor-scarce U.S. economy is merging with a poor and labor-abundant global economy will put pressure on the living standards of U.S. workers for decades to come.

If crafting fairer international rules of the game isn't the answer, what is? Go back to what economics teaches about trade: it increases national income while simultaneously redistributing it. We'd like to keep the increase while making sure the redistribution doesn't leave large swaths of Americans worse off. The way to do this is through *compensation*, and the political and ethical case for this compensation is crystal clear. Global integration is driven by conscious policy decisions made by the government, and its utterly predictable outcome is reduced growth in living standards for many, even most. Just as when a homeowner has his or her house claimed by the government to make way for a public highway, ethical politics demands that compensation be paid to those who have their individual circumstances damaged in the name of the collective good.

Many in the globalization debate have accepted this premise in principle, but the specific compensation measures they endorse are insufficient to meet the scale of the redistribution. Trade Adjustment Assistance (TAA), perhaps the best known program for aiding workers damaged by globalization, provides expanded unemployment benefits and payments for training to workers directly displaced by imports. An oft-recommended supplement to TAA is wage insurance, which would pay import-displaced workers some fraction of the difference between the wage they received at their old job and the wage at new employment.[1] TAA and wage insurance are premised on the belief that the costs of globalization are both small and concentrated, consisting only of the adjustment period when workers displaced by imports have to find new jobs.

This book documents just how much larger the costs of globalization actually are to workers on the losing end. These costs consist not just of jobs displaced by imports but also of the reduced wages for workers subsequently competing with the displaced. The pull of globalization on living standards will get even stronger in the future. The service sector, once thought to be largely insulated from global competition, is beginning to see more and more of its output traded across national borders (accounting services and software programming, say).[2] This offshoring of service work gives globalization a much longer lever with which to affect the U.S. economy, and it has huge potential implications for American workers. The scale of the coming costs from globalization for workers on the losing end requires much more serious thought about the scale of policy responses.

Thinking big

The years following World War II saw an embrace of Keynesian macroeconomics. The enduring lesson of this age was that allowing business cycles to run their course was wasteful, not palliative, and that responsible governments should use policy tools to fight downturns. In the first three decades of the postwar era, macroeconomic policy alone was able to smooth out much of the risk and volatility faced by American households. Hard times in this period generally came to them all at once, in the form of recessions, and good times were shared equally across the distribution of income and earnings.

The commitment to full employment provided much of the insurance against economic hardship that most households needed, both through high and rising wages and employer-based social insurance programs. While this coverage of social benefits and family-sustaining employment was never universal (nor in any way doled out fairly), for decades after World War II the trajectory at least was right and a larger number of workers enjoyed them as time passed.

In recent decades, however, the pursuit of full employment has faltered, and individual outcomes no longer correlate so tightly with the ups and downs of the broader economy as in the past. The breakdown of institutions that shared risk and benefits (unions and minimum wage floors) has conspired with globalization to erode the commonality of economic experience in America.

What the American economy needs today is a policy commitment as big as the embrace of Keynesian macroeconomic policy, a commitment driven by the recognition that there is no *one* American economy anymore. Instead, American households face vastly divergent struggles to carve out a secure economic future for themselves, and they are buffeted by arbitrary events outside their control.

To deal with a harm as large and widespread as globalization has wrought (and has the potential to inflict in coming decades), we need to think more broadly about public policy that re-links aggregate and individual prosperity, a policy that uses all the levers available to a government genuinely concerned about economic security for its citizens: social insurance, public investment, fairer economic rules, and redistribution when other tools fail to provide egalitarian outcomes.

This is not a new idea. The imperatives of globalization have been a primary force for creating and sustaining expansions of the welfare state and social democratic policies across much of the developed world. Perhaps because of chance or because of differences in our politics, this hasn't happened in the United States, and instead we have been content to allow globalization without compensation to proceed apace. This book aims to show just how much this complacency has already hurt us and to spur action to keep the damage from growing.

The first chapter provides a birds-eye view of trends in globalization and inequality in the U.S. economy over the past 30 years. Greater flows of international goods, investment, and people have been accompanied by greater gaps among income levels. The growing gaps are not just the result of the rich getting richer faster, which they have; it's also the result of the middle and the bottom falling.

The numbers tell the story, and these are detailed in Chapter 3, which explains the economic theories underlying the effect of trade flows on wages and examines and updates recent studies that have quantified the magnitude of the effect. But before getting into the hard-nosed economics, Chapter 2 looks at the phenomenon that is hard to quantify but theoretically important: the "threat effect," or the impact on a worker's bargaining position of the *possibility* of having his or her job displaced by imports.

Chapter 4 looks ahead to the potential impact of the relatively new practice of offshoring. Economics has yet to fully examine this phenomenon, but offshoring has the potential to intensify downward pressure on U.S. wages and, by turning comparative advantage on its head, even make the nation *as a whole* poorer.

Chapter 5 estimates in dollars the cost of globalization for the individuals and households adversely affected by it and provides a number of economic benchmarks (the cost of health care, college education, rising energy prices, Social Security reform) to put these costs in perspective. The final chapter sums up and makes policy recommendations.

CHAPTER 1

There's globalization and there's inequality

The United States has experienced a sharp increase in inequality over the past 30 years, and it appears in almost any measure you turn to—individual wages or family incomes, the gap between workers at different points in the earnings distribution, the gap between workers with different educational levels, or the gap between workers with different levels of skill or experience. The haves are having more, and the have-nots aren't.

This rise in inequality coincides with the rising pace of America's integration into the global economy. Over the past 30 years all measures of this integration—flows of exports and imports in total national income, the pace of immigration, and the cross-border flows of capital—have accelerated.[3]

A causal connection between trends in globalization and inequality is in fact predicted by standard economic theory, and there is now substantial economic evidence confirming it. Globalization has contributed to the widening of economic rewards in the U.S. economy. It doesn't explain all of the growth in inequality over the past 30 years, but it explains a significant amount.

Many advocates of the globalization status quo have tried to minimize the inequality-generating impact of international trade by asserting that most of the rise in inequality is generated by other factors. This is true but uncomforting; a fraction of a very large number can still be a large number. If I threw myself into a chasm that was only a fifth as deep as the Grand Canyon, I would still be dead.

The prediction of mainstream economics that globalization generates inequality and inflicts outright harm on the living standards of the majority of American workers is surprising to many well-informed people. The magnitude of the harm is even more surprising. This lack of awareness has well served the political cause of "more trade, period." It needs to be rectified so that we can have serious political debates over how best to manage the American integration into the global economy.

Growing openness

Aside from this growth of inequality, perhaps the single most visible change in the American economy over the past 30 years has been the rise in importance of the international sector. **Figure 1-A** shows the rise of imports and exports as a share of total U.S. gross domestic product (GDP) and the concomitant increase in the trade deficit (the difference between exports and imports). Between 1947 and 1979, the average trade share (imports plus exports) in total GDP was 11%, and it rose by 6.8

FIGURE 1-A. Imports, exports, and the trade balance as a percent of U.S. GDP, 1947-2006

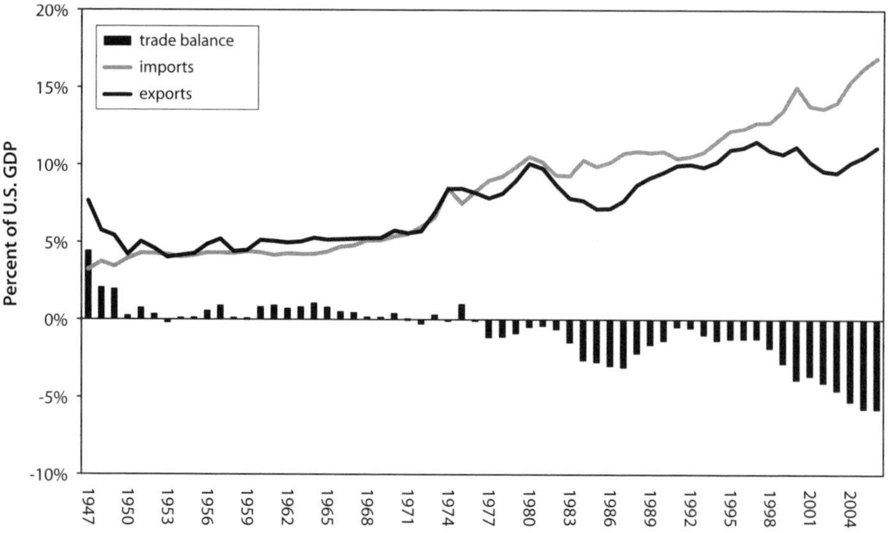

Source: Bureau of Economic Analysis.

percentage points over this time, about 0.21 percentage points annually. Between 1979 and 2005, the trade share averaged 21.3% and stood 9.2 percentage points higher in 2005 than in 1979, an increase of about 0.35 points annually.

Accompanying the acceleration of *total* trade in the latter period was the rise of persistent trade deficits. Aside from a couple of large trade surpluses in the immediate aftermath of World War II, the U.S. economy generally saw balanced trade between 1950 and 1979 (with the trade account averaging a positive 0.3% of GDP). Since then, however, the United States averaged trade *deficits* of 2.2% of GDP, and by the end of 2006 it saw a record deficit of almost 6% of GDP. One thing to keep in mind is that deficits *per se* are not a primary source of wage pressure stemming from globalization. They are problematic in and of themselves, but globalization's wage pressure will persist even when the U.S. economy moves toward more balanced trade.

Most trade was and remains concentrated in manufactured goods, as these have traditionally been the most tradeable parts of the American economy; it's easier to transplant autos from one country to the next as opposed to, say, haircuts. **Figure 1-B** gives an indication of just how tradeable manufacturing output is by scaling manufactured imports and exports against the total domestic output of the manufacturing sector in the United States. As the chart illustrates, the United

FIGURE 1-B. Manufacturing imports and exports as a share of domestic production, and manufacturing trade as a share of total trade, 1977-2006

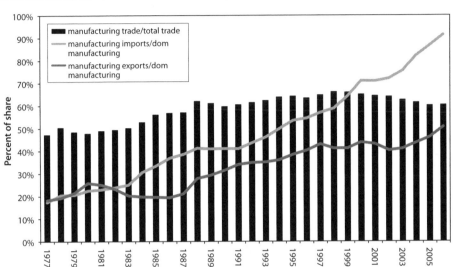

Source: Bureau of Economic Analysis.

States now imports almost as much manufactured output as it produces (the value of imports rose from 21% to 82% of domestic manufacturing output between 1979 and 2006), and it now exports the near-majority of domestic production (the value of exports rose from 21% to 43% of domestic output over the same period).

If technology makes the "travel" of services more feasible, the growing trade-ability of services could mark a new phase of globalization in the near future. Chapter 4 deals with this issue in the context of recent debates regarding the off-shoring of white-collar work.

Manufactured imports and exports constituted over 60% of total trade in 2006 and over 85% of the total deficit. This concentration of the majority of trade flows in a relatively small sector of the U.S. economy (about 14% of GDP is in the manufacturing sector) could be one reason why the perception of globalization's impact on the U.S. economy can vary widely. For workers engaged in manufacturing production, globalization is impossible to miss. For workers engaged in service sector production or government, its impact can be hard to see. Trade theory, however, tells us that globalization affects *all* of these workers.

Is more trade the result of more open trade policy?

While shares of trade in total U.S. GDP have indisputably risen, it does not necessarily follow that U.S. policies have encouraged this expansion. Growing trade shares could have been the result of technological change (lowered transport costs) or political change undertaken outside the United States (more countries joining the global economy).

While technology and developments in foreign governments have surely played a role in increasing trade flows, U.S. policy has also steadily supported this outcome. **Figure 1-C** shows import tariffs imposed by the United States falling steadily between 1971 and 2001, from 4.5% to 1.4%.

While non-tariff barriers and *peak* (as opposed to *average*) tariffs are harder to measure and at least as distorting of trade flows than high average tariffs, it is almost certain that these barriers have similarly declined over time. One piece of evidence supporting this interpretation is the finding by the United States International Trade Commission (USITC) that the economic costs of *all* "significant import restraints" in the U.S. economy, measured as a share of total GDP, were five times as large in 1996 as in 2004. This finding indicates that trade barriers *of all kinds* have fallen rapidly even in the past decade, let alone for the past three decades.

FIGURE 1-C. Effective U.S. tarrifs, 1972-2001

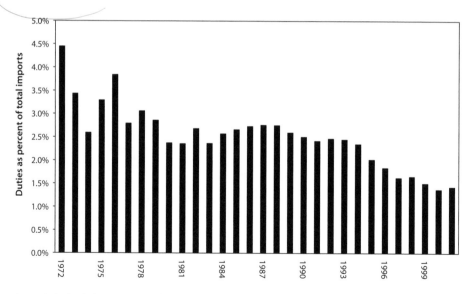

Source: Author's calculations using data from the World Bank.

What kind of trade?

Beginning in the late 1970s and 1980s, economists began examining trade between the United States and nations at similar levels of development, and they posited new theories about why this kind of trade seemed to dominate total flows. The research was essentially focused on questions such as, why do Japan and the United States export and import autos to and from one another? The implications of trade between rich countries (rich/rich trade) for distributional outcomes is far from clear but, on balance, rich/rich trade is more likely than rich/poor trade to be win-win across the broad spectrum of the American workforce.[4]

As less-developed countries' (LDCs) trade share with the United States increased in the 1990s, economists returned to earlier (classical) models of trade to assess the impact of this growth on inequality. While these predictions are treated at length in the next chapter, the essential insight is that trade with less-developed countries (rich/poor trade) leads to the United States specializing in goods whose production results in increased demand for skills, credentials, and capital and reduced demand for less-skilled labor, thereby increasing already-present income differentials. In short, it is this pattern of trade (growing imports from less-developed countries that are produced using intensive amounts of labor) that has predictable and adverse (for the United States) effects on distributional outcomes. This pattern has dominated recent trade flows and, for those concerned about inequality, past and future, this is why globalization is worthy of concern.

Evidence on just how important the rise of rich/poor trade has been for the United States is provided in **Figure 1-D**, which shows the relative incomes of U.S. trading partners, weighted by their shares of total exports and imports.

The relative incomes from Figure 1-D include a group of 32 countries that collectively account for over 90% of total U.S. trade (both imports and exports) in each year under investigation. In each year, the country's share of exports or imports is multiplied by the ratio of its productivity to that of the United States. The sum of these contributions is displayed in the figure; it essentially merges all of these countries into one "import" or "export" aggregate than can be compared to the United States.

This figure shows how the income of U.S. trading partners has either caught up with or lagged behind U.S. income growth. Weighted by exports, the income of countries the United States trades with has shown little trend over time and was actually higher in 2005 (56.7%) than it was at any time since 1973 (the first year investigated), when export-weighted relative incomes were 57.2% of the United States. While the United States is clearly rich relative to the destination countries of its exports, the income gap has slightly fallen over time.

The story is different for imports. The import-weighted relative income of U.S. trading partners has declined rapidly since the beginning of the 1990s, falling from 56.4% in 1989 to 51.0% in 2000 to 49.0% in 2005. This may be a little more surprising than it sounds. While some poor countries (say Mexico) have become more

FIGURE 1-D. Relative incomes of U.S. trading partners

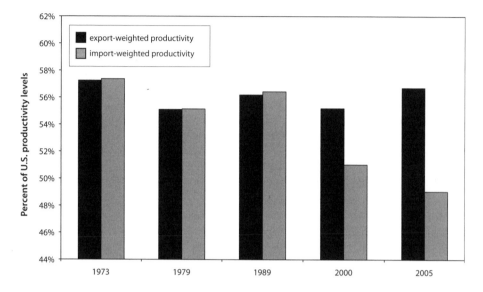

Source: Author's calculations using data from UC-Davis Center on the International Economy and the Penn World Tables.

important trade partners in recent years, dragging down the income average for nations from which the United States imports, poorer countries have *always* been coming into the U.S. import mix. Indeed, many of today's rich countries (such as Germany, Japan, and Italy) were once as poor relative to the United States as Mexico is today. Whether it is surprising or not, it is an extremely relevant fact to the trade and wages debate that the United States now imports from a relatively poorer set of trading partners than it once did.

The overall pattern of the figure, with export-weighted incomes slightly growing and import-weighted incomes noticeably falling, owes much to the fact that China enters with a very small share in exports but a large share in imports. China is essentially bigger and poorer than any trading partner the United States has previously seen, and its entry into the equation is a prime reason why concerns about the implications of rich/poor trade have resurfaced in the globalization debate.

Growing inequality

Coinciding with the growth of the importance of trade flows since the late 1970s for the U.S. economy has been a dramatic increase in economic inequality. Krug-

FIGURE 1-E. Family income growth, 1979-2005

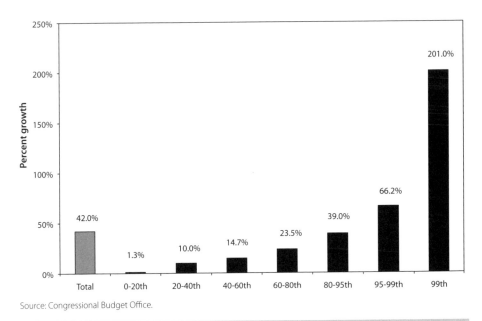

Source: Congressional Budget Office.

man (1992) called the inequality that characterized the late 1970s and 1980s "essentially fractal," meaning it could be seen no matter how one cut the data. Since then, the patterns have become slightly more complex.

Family incomes

The broadest measure of inequality looks at the real, pre-tax earnings of families over time. **Figure 1-E** shows 1979-2005 growth in this measure for various points in the income distribution. The pattern is stark: the lower in the distribution a family sits, the smaller the income gain. Further, only at the 95 percentile and above do family incomes begin exceeding the *average* gain—a testament to just how concentrated income gains were during this period.

Inequality in the wage structure

Even though income growth for most families has lagged behind the average, family income actually provides *too rosy* a view of what has happened to working Americans over the past 30 years. Most family income growth has been the result of longer hours of work, not increases in hourly pay. **Figure 1-F** shows the average annual hours worked by married couples (age 25-54) with children. While husbands' hours

FIGURE 1-F. Annual working hours for marrried couples with children

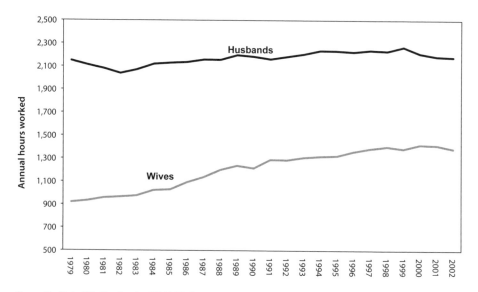

Source: *The State of Working America* 2004-2005, Figure 1T.

FIGURE 1-G. Real hourly wage growth, 1979-2005

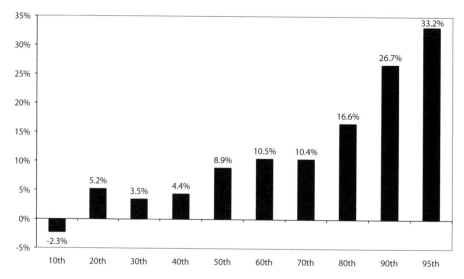

Source: *The State of Working America* 2006-2007, Table 3.4.

have ticked slightly upward during this period, annual hours worked by wives are up over 50% from 1979 to 2002.

If incomes are barely exceeding stagnation even though hours worked are rising briskly, what does this mean for hourly earnings? **Figure 1-G** shows the growth in real (inflation-adjusted) hourly wages for different points in the distribution of wage earnings. From 1979 to 2005, much like family income, only the top 10% of wage earners saw wage gains higher than the average, and families below this range saw annual real wage increases of less than 0.25% per year.[5]

Looking at sub-periods reveals some interesting patterns (**Figure 1-H**). The years 1973-79 saw decent wage gains at the very bottom of the distribution but weak (and even negative) wage performance far up into the distribution—the top 5% saw outright wage declines over this period. The period 1979-89 is more straightforward: it was a wage disaster for workers at the bottom, and then wage growth climbs like stairs to the top of the distribution—though anyone below the 50th percentile was still locked in the basement. The years 1989-2005 look more 1970s-ish at the bottom and middle, with decent gains at the very bottom and more middling gains across the broad middle of the distribution. For top earners, however, the 1980s never end, and their wages grow rapidly through the 1990s and early 2000s. The faster growth at the top and bottom relative to the middle has been dubbed the *polarization* of the earnings structure by Autor et al. (2004).

FIGURE 1-H. Real hourly wage growth over business cycles

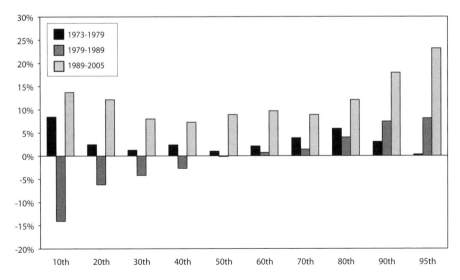

Source: *The State of Working America* 2006-2007, Table 3.4.

FIGURE 1-I. Real hourly wage growth by education, 1979-2005

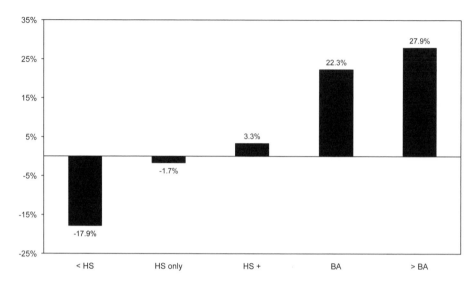

Source: *The State of Working America* 2006-2007, Table 3.17.

Unsurprisingly, the same basic pattern persists when looking at wage growth by educational category. **Figure 1-I** shows wage growth from 1979 to 2005 for workers with less than a high school degree, a high school diploma only, a high school diploma with some college attendance but short of a bachelor's degree, and those with at least a B.A. Between 1979 and 2003, those workers without a high school diploma saw outright (real) wage losses, while those with a diploma and no college attendance saw essentially zero wage growth. Workers with a diploma plus some college saw anemic wage gains (5% over 26 years), while only those with a B.A. and/ or an advanced degree were able to post gains anywhere near 1% per year. Even among this last group, wage gains still lagged behind productivity growth.[6]

Inequality among workers with similar education or experience

Rising inequality among educational groups is an important aspect of the growth of inequality over the past quarter century. However, it misses an important trend— the growth of within-group inequality.

The past 25 years have not just seen college graduates gaining at the expense of non-college graduates. Rather, wages have become more unequal even within each educational category, and this is true even if one controls for labor market experience. College wages are pulling away from non-college wages, and wages within the

FIGURE 1-J. Share of corporate profits in gross domestic income (GDI), 1947-2007

Source: Bureau of Economic Analysis.

universe of college graduates (and non-college graduates) are pulling apart as well. In fact, this within-group inequality can account for at least half of the total rise in American inequality over the past quarter century.

Capital and labor incomes

A last dimension of inequality regards the split between *labor income* (wages and benefits) and *capital income* (profits and net interest). Rising inequality in what is called the distribution of *factor* incomes has received much less attention than the trends for income or education groups, and there are a couple of reasons for this general lack of interest.

First is the observation that this distribution has been generally stable over time. Paul Krugman, in a 1996 book review, noted that "...the share of wages and benefits in national income has been remarkably steady (at about 73 percent) for the past generation" (Krugman 1996).

This description is true, but not totally complete. **Figure 1-J** shows the share of corporate profits in gross domestic income (GDI) in the post-World War II period. Behind the year-to-year jumps is a pronounced shift toward a lower profit share in the post-1973 period. Between 1947 and 1973, the average share of profits in GDI was just over 10%, while between 1979 and 2000 the average share barely reaches over 7%.

Since 1979, although the share rises overall from about 6% to about 9% in 2007, there are lots of ups and downs, and it's hard to see a pronounced trend one way or the other in profits' share of GDI. Simple business cycle averages suggest a small increase in the profit share; it averaged 6.6% from 1979 to 1989, 7.4% from 1989 to 2000, and 7.5% from 2000 to 2006.

There are more than a couple of problems, however, with looking at simple shares of corporate profits in GDI. First, the rise in the profit share has come during a time of rapid educational upgrading (or human capital investment) on the labor side of the equation in the U.S. economy. Between 1979 and 2005, the share of all workers without a high school degree fell by almost 18 percentage points (from 28.5% to 10.6%), while the share with at least a B.A. has almost doubled, rising by almost 15 percentage points (from 14.6% to 29.1%). This rise in human capital investment should have, all else equal, led to an increase in labor's share.

The Bureau of Labor Statistics implicitly tracks the degree of improvement in labor quality in its productivity measurement program. Comparing the raw hours-worked measure with the hours-worked measure adjusted for improved labor quality from 1987 to 2004, one sees a pronounced increase in the human capital stock of American workers, with the "quality-adjusted labor force" growing more than twice as fast as the growth in pure labor hours.

This human capital investment (which is exactly what American workers are constantly advised to undertake in order to share in the fruits of productivity growth) has not garnered workers a larger share of the pie in the post-1979 period, however.

At the same time, there has been a corresponding *decline* in the stock of physical capital relative to the larger economy. This *capital to output* ratio (the value of the physical capital stock divided by GDP), after growing sharply in the first few decades after World War II, has not increased over the past 20 years, and has in fact shrunk slightly over time. This falling ratio should have led to a *decline* in the profit share. If, for example, the capital to output ratio had remained at its 1979 level, the profit share, all else equal, should have fallen 0.53% between 1979 and 2000. In short, a number of pronounced trends that should have raised labor's share over the past decades have failed to do so, leading one to imagine that there are indeed economic forces at work pushing a greater share of economic output toward capital incomes.

Figure 1-K shows the path of labor and capital income share in the *corporate sector* in the postwar period; this analysis avoids some of the anomalies that can arise in using data that includes income that is hard to apportion between labor or capital.[7] Much like the earlier examinations, the profit share looks roughly stable (albeit volatile) after the large fall during the full employment boom of the 1960s.

However, a stable profit *share* can still be consistent with a rising *return to capital,* or *profit rate.* **Figure 1-L** shows the profit rate over the 1952-2006 period. The *profit rate* is profits divided by the corporate capital stock; it is the return to capital services, and it is much more analogous to hourly wage rates than is the

FIGURE 1-K. Capital and labor income shares in U.S. corporate sector, 1947-2007

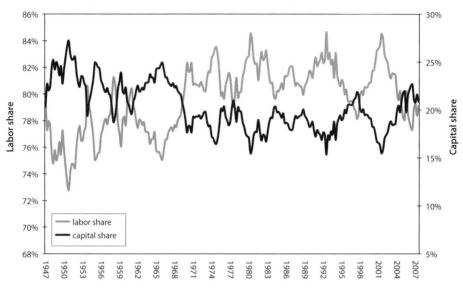

Source: Bureau of Economic Analysis.

FIGURE 1-L. Profit rates in the U.S. economy, 1952-2006

Source: Author's analysis using data from the Bureau of Economic Analysis and the Federal Reserve; sample restricted to non-financial corporate business.

profit share. The figure shows less clear-cut stability over time than do the data on profit *shares*. While both series are volatile, there is a small but steady rise in the profit *rate* post-1980.

There is one last reason to resist thinking that there is no room for distributional concerns regarding labor and capital incomes. First, there has been a huge concentration in the very highest slice of wage earnings in the U.S. economy over the past quarter century. To take just one example, average compensation for top corporate officers has risen over 200% since 1993, according to Bebchuck and Grinstein (2005). Given that a large portion of compensation for these corporate officers consists of bonuses and the exercise of stock options, both of which are tied tightly to corporate performance (profitability), it's far from clear that these earnings are properly classified as labor instead of capital income.

The steady rise in the ratio of incorporated to unincorporated self-employed workers and business owners in the last quarter century would also tend to obscure distinctions between labor and capital incomes. Krueger (1997) cites the example of two doctors who are partners in a business practice. If the business is unincorporated, their incomes are counted as proprietors' income, and traditionally economists have relied on rough rules of thumb to apportion this income between labor and capital earnings. If the doctors incorporate, and begin drawing salaries from the corporation, *all* of their income would henceforth be classified as labor compensation solely.

Conclusion

Two notable trends of the past 30 years in the U.S. economy are a sharp rise in the inequality of incomes and the increasing importance of the international sector. Even though mainstream economic theory predicts a causal link between these trends, economists have been quick to dismiss globalization as a key factor driving rising inequality.

Chapter 3 presents the argument for causality, grounded both in numbers and economic theory. But first, we take a foray into an area of the trade and wages debate where the numbers don't yet lead us, to look at the "threat effect."

CHAPTER 2

The hard to measure, hard to deny, threat effect

The essence of the textbook approach to the causal connection between the growth in trade flows and the growth in inequality is to measure the net outcomes resulting from the churn that trade applies to product and labor markets. For example, the most common method of measuring trade's impact simply counts the number and type of jobs embodied in the production of imports and exports to infer the impact of trade on the supply and demand of various groups of workers. These estimating techniques add much to our views of why and what the U.S. economy imports and exports and how this pattern of trade affects U.S. workers. But focusing solely on how imports and exports add to or subtract from labor supply and demand can miss other important channels through which globalization affects American wages. One clear example of what a broader analysis should also encompass is the *threat effect* of globalization on workers' *bargaining power*.

As was discussed in Chapter 1, ample evidence exists that workers who closely resemble each other based on a range of characteristics that affect pay (age, gender, ethnicity, experience, education) are actually paid differently, and that this *within-group* inequality has increased markedly over the past couple of decades. Many theories have been put forward to explain this trend. The simplest is content to ascribe differences in wage outcomes to differences in "unobserved skill." But a range of studies (that have yet to be integrated into the trade and wages debate) have shown that a substantial portion of the variance in workers' pay is systemically linked to differences in their bargaining power.

These studies posit that frictions in labor markets may give rise to market power, accruing to either employers or employees or both. Take the example of job-specific skills: as a worker stays with a specific employer, she is likely to pick up institutional knowledge and recognize opportunities for institutional efficiencies that make her more valuable to her employer than an outsider (even one with a similar education and work background) would be. Thus, her employer cannot replace her readily with someone from the wider labor market. But there is a downside for her: these job- and employer-specific skills will not generally translate into value (and presumably pay) with any employer aside from her present one.

These job-specific skills constitute an economic rent—value that cannot be purchased on the outside market. The distribution of this rent between the worker and her employer is where bargaining power comes in. Who has the better fallback position if bargaining breaks down and she walks away or is fired from her present job? It is not unreasonable to assume that, in general, the broadened access to outside (i.e., foreign) labor markets made possible by globalization will tip this balance in the employer's favor, if ever so slightly. But this change in relative bargaining power may well not show up in a simple mathematical measurement of trade flows.

An example by Richard Freeman (1995) illustrates how workers' bargaining power is diminished merely by the *threat* of imports, even if no actual imports materialize.

> ...suppose that [a foreign firm] begins producing souvenirs of the Empire State Building and informs souvenir stands [in the United States] that it can provide products at lower prices than U.S. producers. The souvenir stands will then inform American manufacturers that they have to meet the new price to keep their business. The U.S. firms, in turn, will tell their workers that the firms can stay in business only if the workers take a pay cut. If the workers accept the cut, the U.S. firms will maintain their hold on the souvenir market, with no new trade flows. But the threat of trade (like the threat of entry in a contestable market) will have reduced wages in the United States. In this example, the only "footprint" of trade is the change in the relative price of souvenirs.

What does this story tell us about understanding the impact of trade? As Freeman continues, "This is, in stark form, the argument that [measured] trade flows do not accurately reflect trade pressures on the labor market."

In the more mechanical models of trade and wages that dominate the discourse (and even the rest of this book), it is generally assumed that workers with a college degree have been the net winners from globalization in the U.S. economy. The general pattern of U.S. trade is that the United States imports non-college-intensive goods and exports college-intensive goods, thereby reducing demand for non-college-educated workers and increasing demand for college-educated workers. And while the growth in college wages slowed in recent decades, they have still outpaced non-college wages. Further, it's a safe bet that the ability of, say, accountants to buy cheap imported clothes and consumer electronics has been a (generally rare) bright spot for their wages. Accountants generally are not in labor market competition with the workers displaced by imports from low-wage nations, so they have enjoyed the gains from trade (cheaper imports) while remaining mostly insulated from the mechanical pressures imposed by the impact of imports on labor supply and demand.

This said, however, it could well be the case that threat effects provide either an additional channel that reinforces this bias of trade, or a channel that harms wages for many or most college workers as well, leaving only those workers in the most privileged bargaining positions free from downward wage pressure. The avalanche of stories about the practice of offshoring white-collar jobs to low-wage locales that appeared in 2003 and 2004 most likely provided a powerful threat effect even to relatively well-educated workers. It is not hard to imagine that the *Business Week* cover story, "IS YOUR JOB NEXT? The New Global Job Shift," which detailed the exodus of highly skilled jobs from the United States rattled more than a few white-collar workers at Dell or H&R Block

All in all, though, while it may make sense that (1) bargaining power is a key part of wage setting, (2) changes in the bargaining power of various groups in the U.S. economy in recent decades have had large effects on the equality of economic outcomes, and (3) the threat effects of globalization are an important source of change in bargaining power, these assertions are notoriously hard to quantify. So the rest of the book largely proceeds by referencing just the mechanical (but measurable) impacts of globalization on supply and demand in labor markets. If it is true that the threat effects of globalization exacerbate these supply and demand developments, then the estimates referenced in this book as to the cost of globalization for the broad cross-section of American workers should be taken as a lower bound.

CHAPTER 3

Theory and practice: predicting and estimating trade's effect on wages

It should not be surprising, especially to economists, that inequality and trade flows have risen in tandem. Economic theory, after all, predicts exactly such a pattern, with rising trade flows driving greater inequality. Still, many commentators and even many economists seem unfamiliar with this prediction.

Reflecting the predictions of the textbook, debate among researchers who have delved deeply into this topic is generally not a disagreement about the *direction* of trade's influence but rather an empirical argument about the importance of its contribution to the historic run-up in inequality seen over the past couple of decades. On this second issue, there is a wide range of opinion; some economists think trade explains a major portion of the rise in inequality, others believe that it explains very little. A large majority argues that trade contributed somewhere between 10% and 40% of the total rise in inequality in the 1980s and early 1990s.

Framing the question in this way, as "what share of the total rise in inequality over a given period can be accounted for by rising trade flows" is a centerpiece of the trade and wages debate. But this frame can be misleading because the rise in total inequality has been so large that even non-majority contributors to it can have large impacts on workers' incomes. The question can be confusing for another reason: many readers (both laypersons and professionals) are not clear about the underlying trends in inequality. **Table 3-1** provides a summary measure—wages by education.

As the third section of the table shows, wages for workers with a B.A. degree or greater actually fell slightly relative to other workers between 1973 and 1979 before rising rapidly through the 1980s and 1990s. This relative wage remained almost flat in the 2000s, rising only slightly. By 2006, workers with at least a four-year college degree earned wages 88% higher than workers without a degree.

Table 3-1 also shows a basic estimate of the college "premium"—the wage advantage of four-year degree-holders that persists even after controlling for a range of other factors (age, race, ethnicity, marital status, and region of residence). This college premium followed roughly the same pattern as the unadjusted relative wage, falling between 1973 and 1979, rising rapidly throughout the 1980s and 1990s, and ticking up slightly in the 2000s. Even after accounting for other determinants of wages, the wages of workers with at least a four-year college degree were roughly 50% higher in 2006, compared to roughly 30% higher in 1979. This book will follow the general practice by discussing this college premium as the most relevant measure of wage inequality.

TABLE 3-1. Wages by education (in 2006 dollars)

	1973	1979	1989	2000	2006
Average hourly wage					
Less than high school degree	$13.45	$13.69	$11.70	$11.01	$11.19
High school degree only	$15.42	$15.37	$14.26	$14.81	$15.06
High school plus some college	$16.60	$16.43	$16.02	$16.84	$16.84
B.A.	$22.49	$21.54	$22.46	$25.86	$26.28
B.A. plus	$27.18	$26.30	$28.95	$32.70	$33.58
Employment shares					
Less than high school degree	28.5%	20.1%	13.7%	11.1%	10.6%
High school degree only	38.3%	38.5%	36.9%	31.8%	30.6%
High school plus some college	18.5%	22.8%	26.0%	29.6%	29.7%
B.A.	10.1%	12.7%	15.6%	18.8%	19.7%
B.A. plus	4.5%	6.0%	7.9%	8.8%	9.4%
Average wage, two main educational groups					
Less than B.A.	$15.02	$15.25	$14.40	$15.06	$15.25
B.A. or greater	$23.90	$23.10	$24.60	$28.00	$28.60
Relative wage (college/non-college)	1.59	1.51	1.71	1.86	1.88
College premium*	36.3%	29.5%	41.4%	49.0%	49.7%

*Premium based on regression of two education categories (less than B.A. and B.A. plus) and controls for race, gender, ethnicity, region, marital status, and a quartic for age.

Source: *State of Working America* 2006/2007.

The remainder of this chapter provides a rough estimate of the distribution of empirical findings from the trade and wages literature, with a particular focus on three methods of empirical investigation that have defined best practices in the debate. Finally, these best practice methods are applied to more recent periods to get a sense of just how much trade is affecting wages today.

Mainstream trade theory and inequality

Comparative advantage

To get the full flavor of what mainstream economics argues regarding trade and inequality, we start with the most basic insight—*comparative advantage,* the corner-stone of classical trade theory. Take the case of China and the United States. The logic of comparative advantage argues that reducing barriers to trade allows each country to specialize in what it does *relatively* more efficiently. "Relatively" is the crucial word here—even if production costs were lower in China for *both* clothing and aircraft (they are not—the U.S. productivity advantage in aircraft dominates the wage costs), China would still do best specializing in clothing, as its cost advantage is much larger in this more labor-intensive industry. The great contribution of comparative advantage is in proving that this division of labor is a benefit to both countries.

Borrowing a classic textbook example, imagine a lawyer who is expert in providing legal services but also types slightly faster than her secretary. Should the lawyer cut back on providing legal services to do more typing? No—doing her own typing means giving up time that could be devoted to legal work. It makes intuitive sense that giving up (presumably well-paid) legal work for typing seems like a bad idea. But suppose also that the secretary has the skills to write legal briefs, but they take him a lot more time because he doesn't have the legal training of the lawyer. Should the secretary cut back on typing and do more legal work? The answer (perhaps surprisingly this time) is again no.

To see why, start with a couple of radical-sounding assumptions: legal and typing services are the only two goods in the economy, and everybody needs some of each. Say that the secretary can either write two legal briefs in an hour or type 50 pages, and the lawyer can write three legal briefs or type 60 pages. Looking at the relevant cost of legal work as foregone typing (and this is indeed the relevant cost—remember that these are the only goods in the economy), then it makes sense for the secretary to specialize in typing. Each legal brief "costs" the secretary 25 pages of foregone typing. The lawyer, however, can provide each legal brief for only 20 pages of foregone typing.

Essentially, the secretary can "buy" a legal brief from himself at the cost of 25 pages of typing or he can buy the brief from the lawyer for only 20 pages of typing. As long as he needs both legal services and typing, he is better off specializing in relatively poorly paid typing. For the real world application if this example, replace "typing" with labor-intensive apparel production, textile production, call center operations, and furniture production, and replace "legal work" with capital-intensive software, accounting services, high-technology products, and aircraft. Next, swap China for secretary and United States for lawyer.[8]

Hecksher-Ohlin theorem

Comparative advantage explains *why* it makes sense to trade. The workhorse model examining the *patterns* of trade flows (i.e., why the United States imports some goods and exports others) between the United States and poorer nations is the Hecksher-Ohlin theorem (HOT). The HOT and its spinoffs are often referred to more generally as the *factor proportions* approach to trade.

The HOT begins by identifying each nation's endowment of *productive factors*. The original version of the HOT was framed in terms of capital and labor as the productive factors. Recent work on the trade and inequality debate, driven by the perception that inequality had widened predominantly *within* wage incomes in the United States, began framing the HOT and related theorems as being about *skilled* and *unskilled* labor.

For this book, in the name of both brevity and avoidance of the normative baggage of *skilled* and *unskilled*, we identify the factors of production as *labor* and *professionals*, with the latter group supplying credentials, skills, and management services in addition to the labor that is supplied by both groups. These labels are by no means perfect either –production workers often have specialized skills or credentials they apply to their work, and professionals "labor"—but hopefully these labels create an intuitive picture that will make reading easier, plus they avoid the pejorative implication that 70% of workers in the United States—the approximate share without a college degree—are unskilled.

Given their endowment of productive factors, nations can be identified as either professional or labor abundant. Professional-abundant nations (the United States) have, naturally enough, access to relatively cheap professional labor services. Professional abundant nations are by definition labor scarce, and vice-versa. Given a ranking of labor- or professional-abundance, the HOT predicts that exports of professional-abundant nations will be professional-intensive (since these are the goods that these nations will have the comparative advantage in producing), and imports of these nations will be labor-intensive.

These relative weights of professional- and labor-abundance don't mean that (say) laborers have to constitute the *majority* of the workforce for a country to be considered labor-abundant. If the United States has 100 million laborers and 30 million professionals, while Mexico has 50 million laborers and 5 million professionals, between the two the United States is the professional-abundant country, even though laborers constitute the majority of its workforce.

The HOT bottom line is that professional-abundant nations (like the United States) will export professional-intensive goods and import labor-intensive goods.

Heckscher-Ohlin spinoffs

Three theories spun off by the HOT relate directly to questions of inequality; they are the Stolper-Samuelson theorem (SST), the Rybczynski theorem (RT), and the factor price equalization theorem (FPET). All three link *factor* prices (wages for workers and professionals) and *commodity* prices (the prices of, say, apparel and aircraft).

The Stolper-Samuelson theorem (SST)

The spinoff with the most direct and general relevance to the issue of trade and inequality is the SST, which focuses on the consequences of falling trade costs for a nation's scarce factor of production. The general assumption, again, is that the scarce factor in the United States is labor. The global South is assumed to be abundant in labor and scarce in professionals. The SST demonstrates that reductions in trade costs cause an unambiguous reduction in the real return to a nation's *scarce* factor of production; in the case of the United States this means a decline in labor's wages.

Commentators and some economists often express confusion over this point. Even when they grant that a reduction in costs of trade with a labor-abundant country (say China) will depress the demand for American workers, the lower price of imports is often characterized as potentially fighting the reduced labor demand to a draw in terms of labor's real (inflation-adjusted) purchasing power or at least making the precise outcome indeterminate. This is not the case—the SST demonstrates unambiguously that the scarce factor in the United States, labor, will be damaged in absolute, not just relative, terms.[9]

Rogoff (2005) and Krugman and Obstfeld (1994) sum up the implications of the SST model:

> From a policy perspective, the major result of [the SST] was to confirm the intuitive analysis of Ohlin about who wins and who loses when a country opens up to trade. The answer, as we now well understand, is that the relatively abundant factor gains, and the relatively scarce factor loses, not only in absolute terms but in real terms. Thus if capital is the relatively abundant factor (compared to the trading partner), then an opening of trade will lead the return on capital to rise more than proportionately compared to the price of either good, whereas the wage rate will fall relative to the price of either good. (Rogoff 2005)

> Thus international trade has a powerful effect on income distribution… This means that international trade tends to make low-skilled workers in the United States worse off—not just temporarily but on a sustained basis. (Krugman and Obstfeld 1994, 78, 79)

For a more thorough explication of how the SST works, Appendix 1A walks through some of the math.[10] As an example of the application of this theory, start by dividing workers in the United States into labor and professionals. Assume further that there are two sectors in the U.S. economy, apparel and aircraft. Labor and professionals can work in either sector.[11] Lastly, assume that producing each $1 of apparel takes a ratio of labor to professionals twice as high as producing each $1 of aircraft—that is, apparel is the more *labor-intensive* business.

Now, say that falling trade costs (a tariff cut, for example) reduces the price of imported apparel by 10%. In a competitive economy, this means that the price of domestically produced apparel must fall by 10% as well. The upshot of this is that fewer domestic producers are willing to make apparel, as falling prices make it a less attractive business. Imports rise to replace this lost domestic production. Lastly, and importantly, aircraft exports rise as domestic investment once ploughed into apparel looks for new opportunities.

Every $100 of domestic apparel production that is abandoned means that the ratio of labor to professionals laid off by apparel makers is too high to be absorbed in the aircraft sector at labor's going wage. After absorbing all of the professionals released from apparel, there will still be many laborers who cannot find employment in the aircraft sector. If these laborers want a job, they must agree to a wage cut. Further, it's not just the *unemployed* laborers that take wage cuts—*it's all laborers economy-wide*. Incumbent laborers in either industry not agreeing to this wage cut will be replaced by unemployed laborers. These economy-wide wage cuts for laborers are the *gross losses* from trade.

The process works in reverse for professionals. The apparel sector doesn't shed enough of them at the going professional wage in order to meet the extra demands of aircraft production. This imbalance bids up their wages, and these higher wages for professionals constitute the *gross gains* from trade.

As labor has become cheaper relative to professionals, both aircraft and apparel producers will have incentives to adopt new production techniques that economize on professionals and more intensively use labor until the last unemployed worker is absorbed. So, at the end of the adjustment to the tariff cut, the apparel industry has contracted, the aircraft industry has expanded, labor's wages have fallen, professionals' wages have increased, and both industries have a higher labor share than they did before. From the HOT, we also know that gross gains are greater than gross losses, leading to net gains from trade.

These are the standard predictions of mainstream trade theory. Note what this theory does not say: that a damage stemming from globalization is the *adjustment* cost of laborer's unemployment spells between jobs. This temporary adjustment cost is not factored into the SST; rather, the damage specified is the permanent wage loss suffered by *all* labor in this economy.

Something else the theory does not say is that lower prices for apparel provide partial compensation for the damage done labor. In fact, the lower price of apparel *is the problem* for labor, not a countervailing benefit. Further, these lower apparel costs are also the source of the gains from global integration: the greater the *national* gains from globalization, the more labor's wages suffer.

Lastly, a variation of the following argument has become ubiquitous: *trade lets us keep the good jobs in the United States and sends the bad jobs overseas*. It is easy to see where this impression comes from; in the example above, the United States is left with more aircraft jobs and fewer apparel jobs, and, on average, aircraft pays better than apparel. So it seems like the United States has kept the good jobs. However, this observation reflects confusion between what happens to *jobs* versus what happens to *workers*. More *jobs* are indeed located in the higher-wage sector (aircraft) post-trade, but labor receives lower wages *in both sectors*. The higher pay in the aircraft sector is wholly a function of the higher ratio of (high-paid) professionals relative to the labor employed there.

We know from above that it is the wages of labor, not the wages of professionals, that are forced down. Calculating the precise change in wages induced by falling trade costs is a job for the technical appendix (as it is far from straightforward), but an important punch line of the SST is that the fall in workers' wages is larger than the fall in trade costs. This is known as the "magnification effect," and the intuition runs as follows.[12]

We know that overall prices in the import-competing must fall by 10%, which means that the *average* factor price in this sector must fall by 10%, since competition insures that the price of something is exactly equal to the cost of the factors used in producing it. But, we also know that only labor's wage falls, and, labor accounts for less than 100% of the cost of a good. Given this, if average factor prices fall by 10%, and, professional wages rise, then labor's wages must fall by more than 10%.

If, say, labor accounts for 70% of the final price of a good, and we know the price of this good has fallen by 10%, and we know that the entirety of this 10% fall must come out of the return to labor, then labor costs must fall by at least 10% divided by 70%, or 14%.

The SST, in short, demonstrates that falling trade costs reduce the price of a nation's scarce factor. It further shows, as demonstrated above, that the wage cuts induced in the United States by falling tariffs are greater than the magnitude of the tariff.[13] Finally, the SST combined with the HOT show that the difference between the gross gains to professionals and gross losses of workers is positive, implying *net* gains to national income that are (necessarily) just a fraction of both the gross gains to professionals and gross losses to workers.

The Rybczynski theorem (RT)

The Rybczynski theorem complements some of the SST findings. When the prices of apparel and aircraft can adjust, the RT predicts that an increase in the quantity of one factor (say labor) will lead to falling prices for the commodity whose production intensively uses it (apparel). This sparks an SST-type adjustment of factor returns, driving down the price of the *factor* that is more intensely used in this sector.

Rybczynski originally framed his argument in terms of a closed economy, but one can look at it as a prediction of what will happen when labor-abundant nations (like China and India) are integrated into the world economy and increase the global labor pool. In this case, the RT predicts that the price of labor-intensive commodities will fall as a result of this increase in the global labor pool, and these falling prices will harm labor in professional-abundant nations like the United States.

To test the reasonableness of this theory, think of DVD players, apparel, and call center operations, and consider whether or not the expansion of the global labor pool has reduced their prices. Given it surely has, these price reductions have led to resources in the United States moving out of production of these commodities and into the production of professional-intensive goods. This move sets off the SST chain of causation, leading to a fall in wages and a rise in the return to skills, capital, and credentials. Hence, SST results occur *even without changing trade costs*—wages in the United States fall due to the integration of labor-abundant economies into the global trading regime. This is surely one of the more intuitive aspects of the economics of globalization.

The factor-price equalization theorem (FPET)

The factor-price equalization theorem predicts that trade in commodities causes an *absolute* convergence of factor prices (labor and professional wages) across nations. In the case of labor, the expectation is that this convergence will be the result of the wages in the North declining and the wages in the South rising. The logic of this is much the same as in the SST, but it requires more stringent assumptions than the SST, and most economists take its predictions not literally but rather as a directional effect.

Essentially, to believe in the FPET you have to believe that all prices (of goods and of labor and capital) are entirely set on global, not domestic, markets. Further, you must believe that the United States and China have access to the same production technologies in each good, and that trade is not specialized (each country produces some of each good). Lastly, you have to believe that all goods are tradeable—all production is either a potential import or export. If you believe all of this, then the upshot is that all factor returns (wages of workers and professionals) in the United States and China will converge in *absolute* terms: U.S. wages will fall and Chinese wages will rise until they meet someplace in the middle.

If you think that the literal FPET is a real threat to wages in the U.S. economy, you also have to believe that domestic labor supplies within the United States have absolutely no effect on wages (remember, all prices are set on global markets). As a consequence, you would have to believe that if (say) immigration into the United States doubled the supply of labor (added 140 million to the labor force), U.S. wages would be unchanged. In short, on the issue of U.S. wages, if you're an extreme trade pessimist because of a literal reading of the FPET, then by definition you must be an immigration optimist.[14]

What has research found about the link between inequality and trade?

The attempt to quantify the impact of trade flows on American wages is dominated by three methods: factor content analyses (FCA), product price regressions (PPR), and computable general equilibrium models (CGE).

The first, FCA, uses data on imports, exports, and the characteristics of U.S. workers working in import and export industries to estimate the effects of U.S. trade for different types of workers. Essentially, these studies try to translate, say, $1 billion worth of imports into the corresponding amount of labor, skills, and capital embodied in their production. Labor embodied in imports adds to U.S. labor supply and pushes down workers' wages, all else equal. The same exercise is done for exports, which reduces labor supply and bids up wages. The net effect is then calculated and estimates for what all this means for wages of professionals and labor are obtained.

Because the observed flows of imports and exports are translated into labor and professional equivalents, FCA is sometimes said to be measuring the implicit trade in *factor services*. This should make some intuitive sense; by trading aircraft for apparel, the U.S. economy is essentially trading labor services for professional services.

PPR takes as its starting point the literal predictions of the SST: trade hurts labor when labor-intensive industries see price declines driven by globalization. These studies essentially look at the movement of prices across industries ranked by their labor-intensity. The smoking gun for globalization's impact on wages is price declines that are correlated with labor-intensity across industries.

Lastly, while much less prevalent, CGE modeling has provided some of the best-known results on trade and inequality. CGE models combine accounting relationships, input-output linkages, and economic data (or parameter estimates) to examine how policy, technological, or other external changes will impact economic sectors and interest groups. These models are useful in imposing consistency in economic theory and in suggesting a range of possibilities that could be the outcome of policy or other external change. In the trade and wages debate, CGE models generally examine how rising trade flows will filter through to the wages of various types of workers.

More details on these general estimating techniques can be found in Appendices 1B and 1C, the latter of which summarizes almost 30 studies in the trade and wages literature and gives a rough description of their research methodology and findings. Where possible, the summary backs out a number for how much of the rise in inequality during the period in question can be accounted for by trade. This is not always possible—few of the studies were consciously presented in this way. Of the papers that do make this calculation, however (and including those that find an implicit contribution of zero), the average finding (albeit bound by a large confidence interval) is that trade explains just over a quarter of the total rise in inequality in the period under question. Whether this is a little or a lot is a judgment that has not been subject (as noted by Mishel 1995) to great analytical discipline on the part of the economics profession. Chapter 5 remedies this by constructing much more relevant benchmarks with which to compare the implied wage effect embedded in these numbers.

Factor content analysis (FCA)

When it comes to examining the results of studies using FCA, there is really the work of Adrian Wood (1994) and everybody else. Wood uses FCA to gain his finding that international trade can *by itself* explain the majority of the increase in U.S. wage inequality since the early 1970s; he further claims that it explains significant portions of increasing unemployment in Western European nations. Wood's findings imply an importance of trade roughly four times greater than what most other (strict) FCA studies would argue.

The Wood adjustment to FCA

The key difference between Wood's findings and those of other studies in the FCA literature stems from his argument that traditional methods of FCA radically underestimate the degree to which imports arriving in the United States increase the implicit supply of U.S. labor. Wood (1994) essentially points out that goods produced in less-developed countries (which he shorthands as the *global South*) are much more labor-intensive than those produced in the global North—*including those goods classified by statistical agencies as being in the same industry.*

Take the industry labeled *sports equipment*. Sports equipment is made in both the North and the South. However, in the North, producers make, say, golf clubs, whose production is extremely intensive in professionals and capital. In the South, producers make baseballs, whose production requires almost solely labor. Looking at the Northern (United States) labor demand required for *sports equipment* (the number of workers needed to produce golf clubs) will thus greatly underestimate the number of Northern workers that would be needed to produce imports of sporting goods (baseballs) in the absence of trade. To be sure, if the United States had to produce its own baseballs, it would probably not use production techniques as labor-intensive as those currently used in (say) the Dominican Republic, but it also would probably not use techniques as professional-intensive as those it currently uses to make golf clubs.

To operationalize this insight, Wood (1994) measures the labor-intensity of Southern imports with the labor inputs characterized by *Southern* input-output tables. He does make a further adjustment to account for the fact that some of the North/South gap in the labor-intensity of production would not persist if baseballs had to be sewn in the North (i.e., some of the gap may just reflect generalized technological lag in the South, for example). Even so, Wood's net adjustment greatly increases the measured labor intensity of imports from the South, and it results in trade's impact roughly quadrupling compared to using measures of Northern technology for both imports and exports.

Wood drew sharp criticism for estimating the factor content of U.S. imports with Southern input-output tables. Many called this technique invalid, basing their arguments largely on a strict reading of the HOT that includes the assumption that all nations have access to identical production techniques. Given this assumption, domestic (U.S.) production technology is not just a perfectly fine way to measure the labor content embodied in imports to the U.S. economy, it is the *only appropriate way*.

Somewhat ironically, however, recent work in a research strand outside of the trade and wages debate (measuring the factor content of trade to test the validity of the broader predictions of the HOT) has largely validated Wood's technique.[15] This recent literature argues forcefully that the factor content of trade is, just as Wood argues, properly measured with each producer country's input-output relationships.

There is one caveat, however. Measuring the factor content of trade in the Wood (1994) manner does not necessarily allow a perfect mapping of this factor content into implications for U.S. wages. It gets a little complicated, but a rough summary of this issue is that the Wood adjustment allows one to infer *relative* wage changes pretty easily, but one has to make further adjustments to get the resulting *absolute* changes in wages for different groups.

Essentially, because some imports are not competing with current U.S. production (baseballs in the example above), the ability to import these for less than they could be produced domestically provides potential benefits to *all* U.S. workers. So, even as trade increases inequality, the absolute wage losses suffered by U.S. labor may be less than would be inferred in traditional measurement of FCA.

Within, not just between: regression-augmented FCA findings

Upon reflection, it probably should not have been a huge surprise to find that some key insights of Wood (1994) have been vindicated. Stepping away from strict FCA measurement issues, there's another way to interpret Wood's argument that standard FCA results need adjustment: the true impact of trade must be measured not only on *between-industry* reorganizations of production but also on *within-industry* reorganizations. That is, trade doesn't just allow the United States to shed apparel jobs and gain aircraft jobs; it also allows U.S. firms to shed the labor-intensive portions of *both* apparel and aircraft production and keep the capital- and skills-intensive portions of both industries, just as has happened in sporting goods (importing baseballs and keeping golf club production in domestic markets).

The first round of FCA studies used the domestic (U.S.) industry-average measures of education- and labor-intensity to undertake their factor content calculations. This means that they measure, exclusively, the between-industry impact of trade on labor supplies. Equal values of imports and exports of a given industry (say apparel) will, in these estimations, have zero effect on relative wages. If trade, however, does indeed allow imports and exports *within the same industry* to vary greatly in their labor inputs and to affect labor markets, then traditional FCA will miss much of the impact of trade on labor markets. Further, the fact that intra-industry trade is growing in importance means that traditional FCA will pick up less and less of trade's overall impact over time.

Empirical studies show that a large portion of U.S. trade is actually intra-industry (meaning that, as a nation, we import and export a lot of goods in the same industry). For years, many interpreted this intra-industry trade as necessitating a "new trade theory" (some of this trade surely did require a new theory, which dutifully appeared in the 1980s). The new trade theory generally found benign (or at least ambiguous) effects of trade on intra-national distribution. From this conclusion, intra-industry trade flows have often been ruled out of bounds in assessing the inequality-generating aspects of trade. Implicitly at least, this is precisely what many of the first-round of FCA studies did.

This facile dichotomy of between-industry and within-industry shifts had great influence in the larger academic debate over the causes of inequality. Shifts that occurred within industries were assumed to be wholly free of the impact of international competition. The most dominant alternative explanation of rising inequality was known in the economics jargon as "skill-biased technological change," which posited that some technological influence (computers generally) had bid up the demand for skilled workers *in all industries*. Within-industry movements in relative labor demand were thus seen as evidence for skill-biased technological change and against the influence of trade.

Feenstra and Hanson (1995) made a major contribution to the trade and wages debate (and the larger inequality debate) by reframing the HOT as reallocating labor not just from labor-intensive "import industries" to capital-intensive "export industries," but from the labor-intensive portions of production across all industries. In short, they reclaimed within-industry shifts in labor demand as being within the possible influence of trade. Their subsequent empirical analysis (and work since then) provides strong evidence that their hypothesis is correct: trade, not just technology, is a major influence on within-industry shifts in labor demand. Almost without exception, studies that find a very small impact of trade flows on wage inequality tend to focus on the between-industry impacts of trade exclusively and attribute within-industry changes to domestic forces. Since Feenstra and Hanson (1995), this is no longer a serious methodological approach.

Feenstra and Hanson (1995) tested the within-industry impact of trade flows for the 1980s and found that large increases in the import share of an industry are associated with large declines in the share of the wage bill claimed by production workers (their analog to this book's "labor"). They attribute a full third of the rise in the non-production share of the manufacturing wage bill to rising within-industry trade flows. Other authors have subsequently shown that HOT/SST effects are indeed significant even in finely measured intra-industry trade.[16]

Summing up FCA studies

Taking the simple point average of the various studies using FCA yields the estimate that trade can account for 13-20% (depending on which of Wood's estimates is chosen) of the total rise in inequality over the 1980s and 1990s. This average, however, is the product of many studies that congregate either on the very low or very high ends. The low-end estimates, however, all clearly examine trade as only a between-industry phenomenon and use only the U.S. input-output technology to measure the factor content of trade.

The high-end estimates, conversely, all consciously try to capture trade's within-industry component and/or conform more closely to what theory argues proper measurement of the factor content of trade should look like. Given this, the higher mode samples deserve a lot more weight in determining what FCA tells us about the effects of trade on inequality.

Product price regression (PPR) studies

Slaughter (2000) is by far the best and most comprehensive overview of the methodology of PPR studies. The essential approach of PPR is pretty straightforward: correlations between price changes and labor-intensity by industry are examined to see if the predictions of the SST are fulfilled. An extreme defense of PPR over FCA is provided by Leamer (1998, 2000), who argues that *only* PPR can properly pick up the impact of trade on domestic labor markets:

> It does not matter that trade in manufactures is a small proportion of GDP. It does not matter that employment in apparel is only 1 percent of the work force. What matters is whether or not the marginal unskilled worker is employed in the apparel industry; sewing the same garments as a Chinese worker whose wages are one-twentieth of the U.S. level. Then lower prices for apparel as a consequence of increased Chinese apparel supply causes lower wages for all unskilled workers in the same regional labor pool as the U.S. garment worker. (Leamer 1998)

This is a contested view. A capsule review of the debate appears in Appendix 1E, and Krugman (2000) and Leamer (2000) are the best summations of the opposing views. For now, we will side-step Leamer's absolutism and stipulate that falling relative prices for labor-intensive goods would indeed be a useful bit of evidence suggesting that trade was affecting American wages through SST channels. As the next section makes clear, however, regardless of where you come down on the theoretical dispute, the evidence from PPR studies can really provide only a check on the direction, not the magnitude, of trade's impacts.

Empirical findings from past PPR studies

Some of the largest estimates as to the impact of globalization on inequality have come from PPR studies. Leamer (1993), for example, estimated that the North American Free Trade Agreement (NAFTA) alone could end up costing U.S. production workers thousands of dollars per year relative to a baseline without NAF-TA. Taking his numbers seriously as to the effect of trade on inequality would translate into trade explaining 20-100% of the rise in inequality between production and non-production wages from the early 1970s through 1991.

The roughest summary of the PPR literature is that several regression specifications from PPR studies have congregated around quite large numbers regarding the contribution of globalization to inequality, but the sweep of PPR studies has an even wider distribution of estimates as to this effect than those based on FCA.

The core problem of leaning too hard on PPR results is that the signal to noise ratio of price data is notoriously low, as price data are plagued by measurement error. Further, because small price changes can be associated with large relative wage changes (the magnification effect described earlier), a 2% increase in prices for capital-intensive goods (for example) can generate large effects on the relative earnings of labor and capital but still be easily swamped by measurement error in the data on prices, thus making the effect essentially unobservable to the researcher.

Another problem regards the issue of industry classification. Essentially, the PPR studies use aggregated measures of "industry" in their regressions. If, again, one thinks that the apparel the United States imports is a quite different subset of goods than the apparel produced in the United States, then regressing the change in price of the former on the employment share of (less-skilled) labor of the latter is bound to render misleading answers about the adherence of the U.S. economy to SST predictions.

The sweep of results from the PPR literature is hard to characterize as a group.[17] The bimodal nature of PPR results is even stronger than the FCA results, with researchers using the technique deriving both the largest and smallest conclusions regarding trade's impact on inequality. One thing to note, however, is that, as a general rule, the PPR studies that most closely conform to the predictions of trade theory tend to generate larger and more significant numbers regarding the influence of trade on relative wages than others. For example, a study by Feenstra and Hanson (1999), which expends great time and effort on making sure that data and measurement are consistent, yields some of the most robust and large estimates.

Computable general equilibrium (CGE) models

Studies by Krugman (1995) and Cline (1997) are the two most well-known CGE modeling exercises in the trade and wages debate.[18] The models also display the possible variety in comprehensiveness offered by CGE models: the Krugman model fits in 20 cells on a spreadsheet, while the Cline model contains hundreds of equations and disaggregates dozens of countries and sectors to a painstaking degree.

What all CGE models (both simple and complex) share is the tight relationship between the assumptions built into the model and the outcomes. That is, the results of a CGE modeling exercise never "prove" anything; instead they allow one to get a sense of the rough range of outcomes that are consistent with observed data trends.

In this regard, the great virtue of the Krugman (1995) model is its simplicity and transparency. The details of the model are included in Appendix 1, and this model is also used in Chapter 4 to sketch out some scenarios for what the offshoring of service sector work could mean for the U.S. economy. In a nutshell, however, the Krugman (1995) model merges some stylized facts about the U.S. economy along with assumptions about the magnitude of some key parameters to estimate how much relative wages in the United States would change if there were no opportunity to trade with less-developed countries.

One can quibble with some of Krugman's assumptions but, given that the parameters driving the model results number only in the single digits, it is easy to run through sensitivity checks to see if any particularly idiosyncratic decision on the assumptions drives the results. Generally, the results are robust within a pretty wide band of assumptions that most economists studying the issue would consider reasonable.

Krugman's (1995) conclusion is that international trade flows increased the relative wage of skilled workers relative to less-skilled workers by 3% in 1995, up from essentially zero in the late 1970s. This translates into roughly 10% of the total rise in inequality that occurred between 1979 and 1995.

Cline (1997) picks up the Krugman (1995) model and adds layers of complexity—he separates trade flows out by country, specifies more factors of production than just skilled and less-skilled labor, and allows for a range of influences (domestic and foreign factor supplies, for example) to change over time. His trade and income distribution model yields an estimate that trade can account for well over a third of the increase in wage inequality along educational lines that occurred between 1973 and 1993.[19]

Summing up the earlier studies

The clear preponderance of evidence gleaned from all three major strands of the trade and wages debate (FCA, PPR, and CGE models) demonstrates that trade (as predicted in theoretical models) has measurably increased inequality in the United States. There is, however, a notable lack of precision regarding the magnitude (as opposed to direction) of this effect, and this lack of precision has often been cited as an argument against large trade impacts. This does not follow. Essentially, the estimates range from trade explaining 0% of the total rise in inequality to 100%. The majority of estimates cluster between 10% and 40%.

The simple average of the studies referenced in Appendix 1C (which are a relatively exhaustive group) suggests that trade can account for just over a quarter of the total rise in inequality. However, an even more notable (and much more persuasive) *qualitative* finding of this analysis is that successive methodological refinements and tighter adherence to theoretical predictions within each subfield of measurement lead almost uniformly to higher estimates of trade's impact.

This pattern of results (larger and more pronounced trade impacts as one uses more disaggregated data and more theoretically appropriate estimating techniques) argues persuasively for giving greater weight on the upper end of the range of results. For example, taking the simple average of the most theoretically correct and/ or disaggregated single study in each of the three major strands of the debate, the point estimate of trade's impact on inequality is well over a third.[20]

In short, the lessons of past rounds of the trade and wages debate are a bit clearer than are often presented: the vast majority of studies confirms the theoretical prediction that integration of the poor global and rich American economy tends to exacerbate inequality in the United States, and many of these studies identify trade as one of several significant contributors to the rise in inequality that characterized the 1980s and early 1990s. The estimates of the magnitude are imprecise but, as is well-understood in the profession in almost all other contexts, imprecision is not by itself grounds for assuming zero impact.

Updates to best-practice estimates for the late 1990s and early 2000s

The first round of the trade and wages debate ended in the early 1990s. Part of the dwindling interest can be explained by the fact that NAFTA was the spur for the debate; its passage made this conversation seemingly more academic and less policy relevant. Further, the late 1990s saw the first sustained, across-the-board wage increases in the U.S. economy since the 1970s. Inequality generally stabilized (but did not reverse), and the urgency of explanations for its origins ebbed.

However, wages have many determinants, and just because some (most notably the tightest labor market in a generation) were pushing wages higher, it does not follow that globalization was not still pulling some workers' wages down. Inequality may have stabilized in the late 1990s, but global trade flows accelerated.

Further, as soon as the momentum from the red-hot labor market of the late 1990s dissipated, economic outcomes began briskly pulling apart in the 2000s, with wages in the bottom three-fourths of the wage distribution stagnating. The return to rising inequality begs the question: what has globalization done to American wages since the first round of the trade and wages debate ended?

There is no reason to believe that the effect of trade flows on inequality and American wages has slowed since the first round of the trade and wages debate.

Further, even if trade flows continue to account for, say, the same 20% of the total rise in inequality that was found in earlier studies, then the damage trade has done to the wages of adversely affected workers has grown substantially in recent years. Inequality is a moving target in the U.S. economy, so any single influence on inequality that remains even with its overall growth implies a growing burden for American workers.

It may help here to review just what evidence one is looking for in the trade and wages debate. Factor content analysis is looking for evidence that the United States trades professional-intensive goods for labor-intensive imports. This exchange is the root of downward wage pressure for American labor (as opposed to professionals). If this pattern fails to hold, then trade will not wage inequality through factor proportion channels. Product price regressions simply look for evidence that the price of labor-intensive goods is falling. As prices of goods that employ a disproportionate number of the American labor sector fall, labor's wages fall as a result. Falling global prices for labor-intensive goods like apparel and consumer electronics are key potential sources of pressure on American wages. These first two examinations are essentially yes-or-no tests—is trade having an effect or not. If the answer is yes and we want to know how much of an effect, we turn to computable general equilibrium models.

Factor content analysis of the trade effect today

The first cut at updating the factor content of U.S. trade is shown in **Table 3-2**. The first bloc of rows shows the dollar value of U.S. imports and exports for 1979, 1989, 2000, and 2005. The most striking part of these numbers is the large increase in the trade deficit.

The second bloc of rows shows what might be called the "unadjusted" labor content embodied in these imports and exports—essentially the total employment needed to produce the volume of imports and exports using U.S. technology.

The third bloc uses workers with at least a B.A. as proxies for "professionals" and all other workers as proxies for "labor." This bloc shows the share of the jobs created (or displaced) by exports and imports that are filled by workers with and without a B.A., respectively. To make this calculation, the educational shares for these categories are calculated for each industry, and this average is applied to exports and imports for each industry. These educational shares are multiplied by the total labor content of trade in each industry and then summed. This yields the job market impact of imports and exports for workers within these two educational categories.

The last bloc scales this total number of college and non-college job gained or displaced by trade against total economy-wide employment for workers with and without a college degree. In 2005, trade displaced 2.5% of workers with a college degree and 4.6% of workers without a four-year college degree, implying a 2.1% increase in the *relative* supply of those without a four-year degree (4.6% minus 2.5%).

TABLE 3-2. Trade and jobs: numbers and characteristics

	1979	1989	2000	2005
Trade ($ millions)				
Imports	112,235	379,426	1,012,856	1,288,223
Exports	116,585	272,167	625,892	685,077
Net (exports minus imports)	4,350	-107,259	-386,964	-603,146
Jobs embodied (1,000s)				
Imports	3,412	5,623	10,910	9,936
Exports	3,142	3,615	6,564	4,597
Net (imports minus exports)	269	2,008	4,346	5,339
Share of trade-embodied jobs by education				
Imports				
Less than B.A.	89.8%	85.6%	79.0%	77.8%
B.A. or greater	10.2%	14.4%	21.0%	22.2%
Exports				
Less than B.A.	86.8%	80.9%	76.6%	73.5%
B.A. or greater	13.2%	19.1%	23.4%	26.5%
Net (imports minus exports)				
Less than B.A.	335	1,891	3,590	4,354
B.A. or greater	-66	117	757	985
Economy-wide employment, by education				
Less than B.A.	73,205	82,739	95,544	94,127
B.A. or greater	16,817	25,383	36,373	39,576
Trade displacement as percent of economy-wide employment, by education				
Less than B.A.	0.5%	2.3%	3.8%	4.6%
B.A. or greater	-0.4%	0.5%	2.1%	2.5%
Relative change	0.8%	1.8%	1.7%	2.1%

Source: Author's analysis of Bureau of Labor Statistics and Census Bureau data.

This is not a huge number (although it is far from trivial), yet, as noted earlier in the discussion of the work of Adrian Wood (1994), this could well be a substantial underestimate of the true impact of trade.

To get a rough feel for how much of an underestimate this exercise generates, we can look at the work of Davis and Weinstein (2001), who have used internationally comparable input-output tables to measure the factor content of trade when each producer country's exports are measured with their own input-output coefficients (i.e., as Wood recommends). Davis and Weinstein (2003a) have used this technique to show that the actual factor content of trade in typical OECD (Organization for Economic Cooperation and Development) countries is large and firmly in the direction predicted by the HOT. In 1995, the typical OECD country traded roughly 10% of its labor force and 8% of its capital stock. David and Weinstein's data (generously provided by the authors) show that the United States can be used to show the difference between factor contents measured the typical way versus factor content measured in the Wood (1994) manner, and this is demonstrated in **Table 3-3**.

Using only U.S. input-output coefficients, trade in 1995 essentially left the relative supply of labor in the United States unchanged and reduced the implicit supply of capital by around 2.2%. This led to a 2.2% swing in the relative supplies of labor and capital services (2.2% minus 0.0%). Trade with advanced countries actually *reduced* the supply of labor relative to capital in that year.

However, when producer country technology is used to estimate this factor content, trade increased the implicit supply of labor by 5.8%, and even rich country trade contributed largely to this increase. Trade reduced the implicit supply of capital by only 1.4% using the new input-output tables, but the resulting swing in the relative supply of labor and capital services is over 7% (5.8% minus -1.4%). This is over *three times* as large as the relative swing one obtains from using only U.S. input-output relationships for estimation.

Note that the Davis and Weinstein results are based on older data (1995); the impact and labor-intensity of trade with low-wage trading partners has surely climbed a lot since then. Most strikingly, their study's sample did not include China, an extremely labor-abundant country that has grown enormously in importance as a trading partner of the United States since 1995. From this, one can assume that the gap between adjusted and unadjusted measures of the factor content of U.S. trade is even larger than identified with the Davis and Weinstein (2001) data.

Davis and Weinstein (2001) do not have data on the factor service trade flows of different kinds of labor (workers versus professionals, for example). However, given that skill-intensity and capital-intensity correlate closely across countries and, given that economic theory argues for strong complementarities between capital and skills in production, it seems reasonable to assume that the relative labor supply exchanges largely follow the labor/capital exchange identified in the Davis and Weinstein data. As the authors note, "This suggests that one appropriate interpretation is that our variable labor is a very rough proxy for unskilled or semi-skilled labor. We have little doubt that if it were possible to distinguish highly skilled labor separately for our study, the United States and some of the other OECD countries would be judged abundant in that factor."

TABLE 3-3. Conflicting evidence on the labor and capital intensity of U.S. trade

	U.S. technology		Producer technology	
	Capital stock ($ millions)	Employment (1,000s)	Capital stock ($ millions)	Employment (1,000s)
Imports, all countries	-416,006	-10,284	-276,884	-16,110
Imports, advanced countries	-226,369	-5,822	-203,629	-6,478
Imports, less-developed countries	-189,637	-4,462	-73,255	-9,632
Exports, all countries	-330,329	-10,297	-330,329	-10,297
Exports, advanced countries	-170,762	-3,042	-170,762	-3,042
Exports, LDCs	-159,567	-7,255	-159,567	-7,255
Net (imports minus exports), all countries	85,677	-13	53,445	-5,813
Net, advanced countries	55,607	2,780	-32,867	-3,436
Net, LDCs	30,070	-2,793	86,312	-2,377
Total economy endowment	3,886,869	100,151	3,886,869	100,151

Percent of economy			Relative change			Relative change
Net (imports minus exports), all countries	2.2%	0.0%	2.2%	1.4%	-5.8%	7.2%
Net, advanced countries	1.4%	2.8%	-1.3%	-0.8%	-3.4%	2.6%
Net, LDCs	0.8%	-2.8%	3.6%	2.2%	-2.4%	4.6%

Source: Author's analysis of data provided by Donald Davis and David Weinstein.

In short, the Davis and Weinstein results seem to suggest strongly that U.S. imports are far more labor-intensive, and exports professional-intensive, than unadjusted factor contents would suggest, and that unadjusted factor content calculations radically underestimate just how much trade impacts the relative supply of different kinds of American labor and capital.

A check on these adjustments can be made following the lead of Feenstra and Hanson (1995). They, like Wood, predict that trade flows will exert powerful effects on within-industry education shares, not just move production in the United States

FIGURE 3-A. Changes in labor-intensity and LDC import share across industries

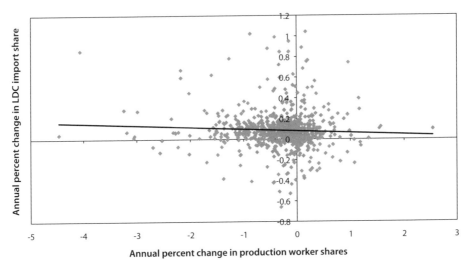

Source: Author's analysis using data from the NBER Productivity Database, the Annual Survey of Manufacturers, and the UC-Davis Center for the International Economy.

between industries. To test this proposition, they examined the 1980s for evidence that rising import shares in an industry are associated with rising import intensity. The intuition is that labor-intensive segments of industrial production can be replaced with imports across manufacturing industries. They find strong evidence of this effect.

Figure 3-A confirms this evidence for the 1990s as well. The scatter-plot shows the increase in the share of each industry's consumption accounted for by imports from less-developed countries and the increase in the share of the wage bill accounted for by production labor. The relationship displayed by the simple trendline is confirmed (and strengthened) with multivariate analysis (shown in **Table A5-1** in Appendix 5), and the magnitudes are similar to those obtained by Feenstra and Hanson (1995) for the earlier time period. In both decades, then, imports really do seem to replace non-college labor in the broad cross-section of manufacturing industries.

Product price regression analysis of the trade effect today

PPR studies have generally looked for evidence that prices have risen more slowly in labor-intensive industries, since trade theory argues that these price declines are the "smoking gun" for trade's implication in rising inequality.

As noted earlier, the PPR studies, while often delivering some of the largest implicit estimates of trade's inequality-generating impact, suffer from problems of noisy data. Product price data are notoriously rife with measurement error. Worse, classical trade theory argues that small price changes are magnified into large changes in relative wages, so the implicit outcomes of these studies depend a lot on small changes in noisy data; this is not a recipe for generating firm results.

As an example, the treatment of one single industry, the manufacturing of computer equipment, has become a sticking point in PPR debates, as its exclusion or inclusion actually has flipped the sign on price regression coefficients. Despite this, it remains worth going over some of the basics of PPR analysis to see if anything in the technique leans firmly against the idea that trade is generating inequality.

Aggregate import/export price indices

The simplest (but a potentially misleading) way to examine the plausibility of trade impacts on inequality is to examine overall import and export price indices for the U.S. economy. If the channel through which trade impacts American wages is falling relative prices for imports, then one should see import prices rising more slowly than export prices over time.

One problem with looking at these aggregate import and export price indices is that both of them are dragged around a lot by volatile commodity prices—the changing price of oil and agricultural products, in particular. Given that the United States is essentially a trivial producer of oil, few would argue that rising or falling oil prices do much to help or hurt American labor through factor proportions effects. The more relevant aggregate measures, then, are the price index for imports *excluding petroleum* relative to the price index for exports *excluding agricultural products*.

Figure 3-B shows these aggregate price indices over time. At first blush, they move consistently with the predictions of the SST; export prices rose 8% faster than import prices between 1989 and 2006. This particular period is chosen because it is as far back as the data allow going while still choosing end-points that are close to business cycle peaks (or as close as we can get contemporaneously). This period also makes sense because the trade-weighted value of the dollar, which swung wildly *during* the period, is actually quite close at the two end-points.

An important final note needs to be made in regard to the examination of overall (or large subaggregate) import prices. Feenstra and Shiels (1994) argue persuasively that import price indices are consistently biased upward, owing to the fact that new goods and new producers (from different, and often lower-wage, countries) are constantly becoming available but are picked up in the price indices only with a considerable lag. This argument has managed to percolate out into the non-academic world, with Mandel (2007) presenting it in recent issues of *Business Week*.

FIGURE 3-B. Prices for non-petroleum imports and non-agricultural exports, 1989-2005

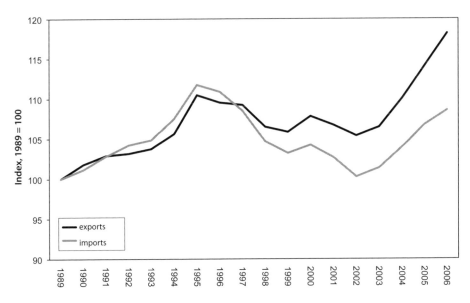

Source: Bureau of Labor Statistics.

Feenstra and Shiels (1994) argue, based on a thorough econometric review of the evidence, that import price indices are biased upward by 1-1.5% per annum. Given that even the (potentially biased) aggregate price data show a slower rise in import prices vis-à-vis export prices, any upward bias in measured import prices makes the case for Stolper-Samuelson effects coming through import prices that much stronger.

Industry prices

Lastly, jumping from a bird's-eye view straight down into the weeds, **Figure 3-C** shows the most theoretically correct price regression that the PPR literature affords (see Appendix 1B for the precise specification). The scatter-plot diagram shows the relationship between industry price growth and the labor intensity of 280 manufacturing industries in the 1990s. The trendline shows the results of a simple regression relating price growth to the share of non-college labor payments in total value-added. The negative relationship (higher non-college intensity is associated with slower price growth) is in line with SST predictions and is based on what Slaughter (2000) has identified as the single most valid regression test of SST predictions. (The slope

FIGURE 3-C. Price changes and labor intensity across industries

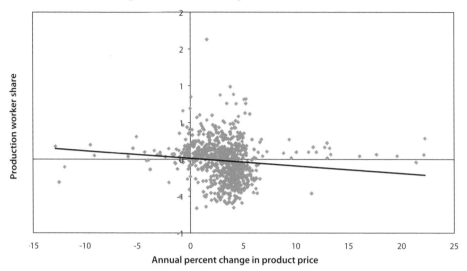

Source: Author's analysis using data from the NBER Productivity Database, the Annual Survey of Manufacturers, and the UC-Davis Center for the International Economy.

of the trendlines identified in the figure is confirmed as statistically significant in some simple multivariate regressions shown in **Table A5-2** in Appendix 5.)

In short, price changes at both the very macro and the very micro level seem to be correctly correlated with industry factor-intensity for SST effects to be at work. Given the fragility of most price regressions, this is a thin reed on which to hang a lot in the trade and wages debate, but it's consistent with the direction of predictions from classical trade theory. It seems clear that import prices are indeed rising more slowly than export prices, and price increases at the industry level are negatively correlated with labor intensity, both of which are strong signals that the direction of trade's impact on inequality is something to worry about.

CGE models

This section builds on what Krugman (1995) termed a "toy" computable general equilibrium model that aimed to quantify the rough magnitude of trade's impact on wages. The mechanics and assumptions behind this model are described more fully in Appendix 1H. The essential features have the United States being abundant in skills, capital, and credentials (referred to collectively, again, as professional ser-vices relative to the rest of the world and also as being labor-scarce. Accordingly, the United States exports professional-intensive goods and imports labor-intensive goods. This exchange bids up the relative demand for professionals and bids down the relative demand for labor, leading to greater inequality.

The Krugman study essentially sets up a model U.S. economy and uses this model to answer two questions: how much would product prices (say apparel prices) have to change to stifle all imports from less-developed countries (LDCs) from coming into the United States, and how much would wages change in response to this hypothetical change? In other words, what would U.S. wages (and product prices) be *but for* the opportunity to trade with LDCs? The full model is specified in Appendix 1. While it is stylized, its results are remarkably robust to changes in the assumptions that underlie it.

The key parameter in this exercise is the volume of trade conducted with lower-wage trading partners. Strictly, the relevant measure is imports from LDCs as a share of U.S. GDP. However, given large U.S. trade deficits over the time period in question, and given that eventually these deficits will have to correct themselves, looking only at imports may overstate the long-run influence of LDC trade. Another plausible measure is the average of imports and exports. The following discussion uses both measures and calculates a high and a low estimate of the influence of trade flows on relative wages. The high estimate uses the share of LDC imports while the low estimate uses the average of LDC imports and exports. The scenario here counts all manufacturing trade from nations outside a core group of advanced countries (the 15 European Union countries plus Australia, Canada, New Zealand, Norway, Switzerland, Israel, and Japan) and scales this value against total U.S. GDP.

Cline (1997) notes a possible reason why the Krugman (1995) model may understate trade's influence on relative wage growth: it assumes that labor and professionals are ready substitutes for each other. This means that Krugman uses a relatively high value for the *elasticity of substitution* between labor and professionals. If it is easy to substitute labor for professionals and vice-versa, then small changes in *relative* wages will induce firms to substantially re-orient their production techniques. This means that any economy-wide "shock" to relative supplies of labor and professionals (technological changes, trade flows, or any other) will be accommodated through labor/professional substitution that happens absent large changes in relative wages. At the broadest level, it's hard to see how rising inequality could ever occur in an economy where labor and professionals could so easily be substituted for each other (and, indeed, if they were *perfectly* substitutable, there could be no change in relative earnings).

Krugman chooses an elasticity of substitution of 1. Cline (1997) argues that it should be lower, perhaps as low as 0.5 (although he settles on 0.7 as his baseline estimate). Cline's view is contested—a number of studies have put this elasticity at over 1.[21] He does, however, make a compelling case that higher estimates of this parameter are not relevant to the trade and wages debate. The following discussion uses both the Krugman and Cline estimates (1 and 0.7) to bracket the high and low estimates of trade's influence on relative wages.

TABLE 3-4. Results from updating the Krugman (1995) model

	1973	1979	1989	1995	2000	2005	1973-95	1995-2005	1973-2005	1979-2005
LDC Share										
Imports	0.9%	1.6%	2.6%	3.7%	5.1%	6.2%	2.7%	2.5%	5.3%	4.6%
Trade	1.1%	1.9%	2.5%	3.5%	4.1%	4.9%	2.4%	1.4%	3.8%	3.0%
Average	1.0%	1.8%	2.5%	3.6%	4.6%	5.6%	2.6%	2.0%	4.5%	3.8%
Relative wage change										
High estimate	1.6%	2.8%	4.5%	6.4%	8.8%	10.7%	4.7%	4.4%	9.1%	7.9%
Low estimate	1.5%	2.6%	3.4%	4.8%	5.7%	6.9%	3.3%	2.1%	5.4%	4.3%
Medium estimate	1.6%	2.7%	4.0%	5.6%	7.3%	8.8%	4.0%	3.2%	7.2%	6.1%
Actual college premium	36.3%	29.5%	41.4%	45.7%	49.0%	49.7%	9.4%	4.0%	13.4%	20.2%
Trade's contribution	4.5%	9.5%	10.9%	13.9%	17.9%	21.6%	50.5%	108.3%	67.9%	39.1%
Absolute changes										
High estimate										
College	0.7%	1.3%	2.0%	2.9%	4.0%	4.8%	2.1%	2.0%	4.1%	3.6%
Non-college	0.9%	1.5%	2.5%	3.5%	4.8%	5.9%	2.6%	2.4%	5.0%	4.4%
Low estimate										
College	0.7%	1.2%	1.5%	2.2%	2.6%	3.1%	1.5%	0.9%	2.4%	1.9%
Non-college	0.8%	1.5%	1.9%	2.6%	3.1%	3.8%	1.8%	1.2%	2.9%	2.3%
Medium estimate										
College	0.7%	1.2%	1.8%	2.5%	3.3%	4.0%	1.8%	1.5%	3.3%	2.7%
Non-college	0.9%	1.5%	2.2%	3.1%	4.0%	4.8%	2.2%	1.8%	4.0%	3.3%

Source: Author's analysis of Krugman (1995) model, using data from the UC-Center on the International Economy and the United States International Trade Commission.

Updating the Krugman (1995) model shows that the large rise in the less-developed-country share of total trade brings with it a large rise in the labor market impact of trade. **Table 3-4** provides the relevant numbers. It shows the share of U.S. GDP accounted for by trade with less-developed countries, the change in returns to labor and skills implied by this share, and the relative change in the returns to labor vis-à-vis professionals generated by this trade. These data are presented for a range of years between 1973 and 2006, and high, medium, and low estimates of trade's impact are given. The high estimate uses the LDC import share and a low value (0.7) for the elasticity of substitution. The low estimate uses the LDC trade (average of imports and exports) and a high value (1) for the elasticity of substitution. The medium estimate is the average of the two.

The results for 1995 are in line with Krugman's estimates. The 1995 findings are included to show that any difference from the original findings is due to data input differences, not a difference in model structure. A slightly higher estimate here for the less-developed-country share of trade (2.6% versus his 2.2%) leads directly to the higher estimates on relative wage changes in this table.

By 2006, this trade share with less-developed countries is more than 60% higher than in 1995, and the impact of trade flows on absolute and relative wages rises accordingly. Trade with less-developed countries raised the relative wage of professionals versus labor by 7-11% by 2006, with labor earnings down by 4-6% relative to a counter-factual of no trade with less-developed countries. Chapter 5 will argue whether this magnitude should be considered large or small, but suffice it to say for now that it's quite a bit larger than most participants in the contemporary trade and wages debates seem eager to advertise.

For our last update to the trade and wages literature, we turn to the 1223 model developed by Robinson and Thierfelder (2002) to estimate the magnitude of trade's effects. The details of the model are specified in the Appendix 1H. It essentially makes room in classical trade theory (the Hecksher-Ohlin theorem, or HOT) for a non-traded sector in the economy. Classical trade theory often generates predictions of large differences between what an economy produces versus what it consumes; this large difference is the inevitable outcome of assuming each good in the economy is either exported or imported. The 1223 model adds a non-traded sector to the HOT. If *all* goods are indeed traded, then the 1223 model collapses into a traditional HOT model.

This large non-traded sector gives the model some appealing features. First, it reflects reality better, especially for a U.S. economy that has a trade share (imports plus exports as a share of GDP) of less than 30%.[22] Second, unlike strong forms of classical trade theory, it allows domestic influences (changing labor supplies, for example) to have significant effects on domestic wages. Third, while it preserves the assumption that it is import *prices* that translate into domestic labor market changes, these changes are mediated by the *volume* of trade. Again, this is surely much more realistic; it certainly matters to U.S. wages if the United States imports 20% of total consumption rather than 2%, regardless of what the price changes are.

The results of the 1223 model boil down to changes in relative wages depending on essentially six influences: (1) the gap between growth of import and export prices, (2) changes in the supplies of various grades of labor (i.e., the relative shares of college and non-college workers, say, in the total labor force), (3) the trade balance, (4) the share of trade in total national income, (5) the difference in labor- and education-intensity between exports and domestic production, and, most important, (6) the degree of substitutability between imports and domestic production.

In their original presentation of the 1223 model, Robinson and Thierfelder (2002) found relatively small results from falling world prices on inequality. There are, however, a couple of reasons to think they may have underestimated trade's impact.

First, they examined only the 1980-91 period. This first period saw a huge run-up in the value of the dollar and a consequent rapid fall in the price of imports in their examination. Given that their import and export price measures go back to 1980, and given that more disaggregated price indices for imports and exports only become available in the mid-1980s, it seems that they are including petroleum and agricultural imports and exports as well, which could be problematic, for reasons alluded to earlier. Second, and by far the most important, they use a relatively low value (3) for their estimate of the "Armington elasticity of import demand." This parameter is crucially important in their model (and in the real world), as it determines how closely imports and domestic consumption compete and hence how intensely falling global prices impact domestic outcomes.

A relatively low elasticity means that imports and domestic production are largely noncompetitive, so falling import prices do not place any pressure on domestic product or labor markets. A high elasticity, on the other hand, means that small changes in import prices lead to a large displacement of domestic production and has greater labor market consequences. The strong results predicted from the classical Stolper-Samuelson theorem are in part the consequence of implicitly assuming an Armington elasticity of infinity.

While infinity is clearly too high (and too hard to model), Ruhl (2003) has powerfully argued that proper specification of the Armington elasticity in this context (long-run, structural changes in the cost of selling imports in the U.S. market) yields estimates much larger than 3. He notes several studies that have elasticities as large as 14—almost five times as large as that chosen by Robinson and Thierfelder (2002). The analysis here uses 7.5 as the Armington elasticity, and it is this change that drives the bulk of the different results between it and the Robinson and Thierfelder (2002) formulation of the 1223 model.

Table 3-5 presents the summary results from using the baseline 1223 model. They show a strong influence of trade on wages in the 1990s. Falling (measured) import prices from 1989 to 2005 increased the college/non-college wage gap by almost 6%.

Using the Feenstra and Shiels (1994) suggested correction to import prices would imply a much larger estimate of import price effects on relative wages and would boost the estimate of the impact of trade (both import prices and the countervailing trade balance effect) on relative wages to over 12% for the 1989-2005 period. Unfortunately, the data requirements of the 1223 model (especially the import and export price indices) do not allow a reliable look back into the 1980s.

TABLE 3-5. Results from the 1223 (Robinson and Thierfelder) model

	1989-2000	2000-05	1989-2005
Induced change in college/non-college wage			
Import - export prices	2.2%	3.3%	5.9%
Changing trade balance	-1.6%	-1.9%	-3.5%
Changing labor force composition	-9.8%	-3.8%	-13.6%
Actual change in college/non-college premium	7.4%	0.9%	8.3%
Contribution to total change			
Import - export prices	29.7%	368.7%	70.7%
Changing trade balance	-21.7%	-212.9%	-42.4%
Total trade effect (sum of above)	8.0%	155.8%	28.2%
Changing labor force composition	-132.6%	-425.3%	-164.3%

Source: Author's analysis using the Robinson and Thierfelder (2002) model and data from the Bureau of Labor Statistics and the Census Bureau.

Conclusion

Both factor content analysis and price studies confirm that the directional impact of trade remains consistent with concerns about Stolper-Samuelson effects on relative wages. The United States still imports goods that are more labor-intensive than its exports, and even at the intra-industry level production that is shed due to import competition is relatively more labor-intensive than production that is retained domestically. Both aggregate and industry prices, even when potentially plagued by upward bias in measurement, are consistent with Stolper-Samuelson effects: import prices have risen more slowly than export prices, and industry price declines are negatively correlated with labor intensity. The computable general equilibrium models suggest that trade flows by 2006 increased the relative wages of college graduates over non-college graduates by between 6 and 12%.

There is one last important point to be made about the framing of these results. Many studies of inequality take 1979 as a starting point, generally because this was the high point of earnings equality in the United States over the past generation. These studies than look at only the *change* in trade's impact and inequality since 1979, and discuss the share of the total growth in inequality since 1979 that trade can explain. Taking the mid estimate of the *change* in trade's impact on relative wages between 1979 and 2005 (6%), for example, implies that it explains roughly 30% of the rise in the college wage premium over that time.

It's far from clear, however, that this is the only useful reference point for the issue of trade's labor market impacts. For one thing, contrary to many people's assumptions, trade with less-developed countries actually grew faster in the 1970s than in the 1980s. Starting in 1979 essentially defines away a significant period of trade's influence on relative wages.

The relevant question is, but for the influence of trade, how much more equal would U.S. wages be today? And this is the political question at hand. If one then wants to argue that this total impact of trade (not just the impact that occurred post-1973 or post-1979) is big or small by scaling it against some other benchmark (say, the total rise in inequality that occurred in the past 30 years), then go for it. But, picking arbitrary start years (especially ones that ignore a decade that saw trade's influence on relative wages grow every bit as fast as the other decades that are generally considered) can provide a distorted picture of how important trade flows are to the U.S. labor market.

CHAPTER 4

The offshoring of service-sector jobs: more of the same, but more so

The focus of trade's impact on American labor markets has to date been centered on manufacturing, as this sector accounts for about 80% of all trade. But in recent years, increased reports of U.S. companies' importing work that was traditionally considered untradeable—such as call center operations, software programming, and various business process services—has led to anxiety over job security across a much wider swath of the American workforce.

Early rounds of the trade and wages debate reached one point of near-consensus: trade's impact on American incomes was bounded by the natural ceiling that was the (relatively) low share of U.S. workers employed in tradeable industries. Some quotes from the mid-nineties give a good indication of how low the ceiling was thought to be:

> In 1993, roughly 15 percent of American workers were employed in manufacturing. The vast majority of unskilled workers were employed producing nontraded goods, such as retail trade and various services. In such a world, it is hard to see how pressures on wages emanating from traded goods can determine wages economy-wide.(Freeman 1995)

> In particular, imports of manufactured goods from developing countries are still only about 2 percent of the combined GDP of the OECD. The conventional wisdom is that trade flows of this limited magnitude cannot explain the very large changes in relative factor prices that have occurred.... (Krugman 1995)

> ...when the large portion of the economy that is nontradeable and the limits of international specialization imposed by home orientation in consumption and production are taken into account, there is much more limited scope for trade to affect relative factor prices. (Cline 1997)

As these authors wrote a decade ago, substantially fewer than 20% of American workers could be plausibly identified as being in competition with workers around the globe. If the new trend of offshoring service-sector work represents (among other things) an expanded number of industries that are now "tradeable," the reassuring tone of the economists quoted above no longer holds, as globalization now has a much longer lever with which to impact U.S. labor markets. Simply

FIGURE 4-A. The 75/25 global economy: national productivity and labor force in 2005

Source: Penn World Tables.

put, if offshoring doubles the number of workers who are employed in industries that are now tradeable, then it may also double the impact globalization has on American labor markets.[23]

Figure 4-A (based roughly on presentations by Ed Leamer (1993)) illustrates the issue. Each point represents a country, and the line segment coming in from the left of each country represents the size of its labor force. The left-most (highest) line segment shows levels of GDP per worker in the United States, and the width of the segment coming from the left to the U.S. "dot" represents the U.S. labor force (roughly 130 million people). As you move from the United States to the right, the line dips a bit, and you run into a group of still-rich but generally small countries: the UK, France, Italy, the Scandanavian countries, and then the not-so-small Germany and Japan.

Before long the line starts to drop precipitously, and you see long line segments (big national labor forces) that have per worker income levels only a fraction of U.S. levels (labeled countries include Mexico, Brazil, China, India, and Indonesia). The figure illustrates that *most* of the global labor force works in nations that are much poorer than the United States. In fact, 75% of the global labor force works

FIGURE 4-B. Productivity and labor force, adjusted for global integration

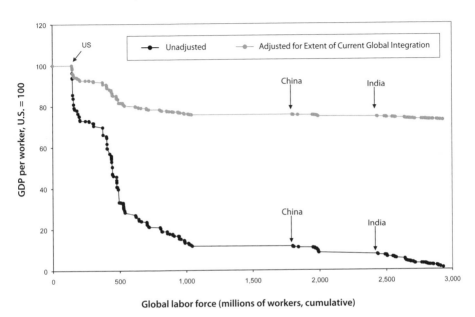

Source: Author's calculations from Penn World Tables.

in nations whose average GDP per worker is less than 25% of that prevailing in the United States. Leamer describes it in this way:

> Think of this figure as if it were a reservoir of liquid with some very high levels and some very low levels. In the absence of dikes to maintain the difference in the levels, the liquid in the high spots would flow into the lower areas, eventually equalizing the level everywhere. This equalization produces lower wages for high-wage countries and higher wages for the low-income countries. (Leamer 1993)

There is, however, something missing from Leamer's description: the degree of *international contestability* between each nation's output. If (to take an extreme example) every country produced only goods and services that were nontradeable (say housing, health care, and haircuts), then these wide differences in productivity and labor earnings would not translate into pressure on high-wage countries. Similarly, if each country completely specialized in what they produced, then, again, wage differences could persist with no pressure on wages in the high-wage region.

Figure 4-B adds an adjustment to these income differences to reflect the fact that only a portion of a nation's output is contested in global markets. A liberal estimate of what share of U.S. output could be traded across national borders is 30%. This leaves over two-thirds of the U.S. economy essentially insulated from foreign competition. Figure 4-B adjusts foreign productivity levels to account for this fact, essentially only allowing 30% of the difference between foreign and U.S. productivity levels to be reflected in the chart.

In this second figure, a given amount of liquid filling in this reservoir would be equalized at a higher productivity (wage) level than in the first figure. The message, again, is that a prime bulwark that protects wages in rich nations against the full force of low-wage competition is the non-tradeability of much of their economies. The offshoring of service-sector work could essentially tear down the levee provided by the large nontradeable sector in rich countries.

The offshoring debate, front and center

The epicenter of the offshoring debate may well have been the February 3, 2003 *Business Week* cover story, "IS YOUR JOB NEXT? The New Global Job Shift" The article's account of the exodus of high-skilled jobs from the United States gave TV business channels, and their economist-guests, something to chew on for months. Among some notable comments were those by Greg Mankiw (then director of the White House Council of Economic Advisors) and Jagdish Bhagwati (a distinguished trade theorist from Columbia University), who both argued strongly that offshoring merely represented the possibility for the United States to conduct more international trade of the same sort that had impacted U.S. manufacturing during the 1980s and 1990s.[24] Since many economists and virtually all economic journalists at elite U.S. newspapers viewed this kind of trade as unambiguously beneficial, these characterizations were thought to effectively allay any fears about the new trend.

The comfort was misplaced. American workers have much to fear from offshoring, even in a best-case scenario in which it represents just more of the same kind of trade. Offshoring has the potential to drag on the growth of living standards of a huge number of American workers for decades to come. The U.S. economy is flexible enough to ensure that jobs are generated for the vast majority of those who want one. But the jobs generated do not necessarily pay as well as the ones preceding them. Generating *enough* jobs is something the U.S. economy does fairly well, even in the age of globalization. Generating enough *good* jobs that enable a secure livelihood is no sure thing.

Combining simple models of international trade's impact on the U.S. economy with a range of predictions about what share of the American labor force will be potentially affected by offshoring over the coming decade allows a rough estimate of offshoring's wage impact. The results (the mechanics of which are discussed below) are discouraging.

Essentially, offshoring could raise the *relative* wages of college graduates vis-à-vis other workers by 12-25%. This is equivalent to 50-100% of the *entire* increase in this relative wage that occurred between 1979 and 2003, compressed into 10 years. Note that this is an increase in relative, not absolute, wages. Further, offshoring could lower absolute wages for workers without a four-year college degree by almost 6-12%, more than undoing *all* wage gains made by this group over the past 30 years.

Note that these numbers are not *forecasts* for what will happen to wages over the next decade—wage growth depends on a number of factors besides trade and offshoring. Instead, they provide a rough range of how much offshoring alone will affect this growth if predictions about its potential reach are accurate.

Winners and losers

This chapter recycles the Krugman (1995) model put to use in Chapter 3 to provide a "back-of-the-envelope" forecast as to how much offshoring could affect U.S. workers. Instead of using historical data on trade flows, the exercise in this chapter uses a variety of *forecasts* about the extent and reach of offshoring over the next decade as inputs into the Krugman model.

Precise data as to even the *current* extent of offshoring of service-sector work are generally unavailable. The data set that should best capture the growing tradeability of a wide range of U.S. industries is the international trade in services report issued by the Bureau of Economic Analysis (BEA). Close inspection of this report, however, shows little evidence of a massive (or even significant) increase in service sector trade in the past decade. Comparison of this report to private sector reporting of specific service transactions, however (like the report by the Indian Software Association, or NASSCOM), provides some suggestive evidence that the BEA isn't quite capturing the increase in international service sector transactions.

Current trends and the potential weaknesses of official data aside, a number of economic researchers and observers have made forecasts as to the number of jobs that could be potentially up for grabs in the future, as technology and policy makes more and more jobs internationally contestable:

- The estimate with perhaps the best pedigree comes from Alan Blinder, Princeton professor and former chairman of the Council of Economic Advisors under President Clinton. Blinder wrote in *Foreign Affairs* that offshoring's impact could mean that two to three times as many jobs could be internationally contestable as are presently contestable in the manufacturing sector, which supplies the vast majority of contestable jobs today (Blinder 2006). In a followup piece with substantially more data-crunching behind it, Blinder scaled back his original estimate, rating 22-29% of the U.S. workforce as *potentially offshorable* over roughly the next one or two decades (Blinder 2007).

- Lori Kletzer and J. Bradford Jensen have one of the most data-intensive and well-specified forecasts. Kletzer and Jensen used the implied domestic trade-ability of various industries and occupations in the United States to measure the possibilities for global offshoring in the future. They estimate that about 30 million jobs over and above those currently contested have the potential to be offshored (Kletzer and Jensen 2005).

- Of the remaining forecasts, the first comes from the consulting and research company Forrester Research (2004), which forecast 3.4 million jobs being off-shored over the next decade. It is important to note that this estimate, unlike the others that follow, is of how many jobs will *actually* be offshored, not how many jobs have the *potential* to be. All other reports in this section forecast potentially offshorable jobs, so we will translate the Forrester number accordingly to derive an apples-to-apples comparison.

- Ashok Bardhan and Cynthia Kroll (2004) have estimated that up to 14 million jobs will be newly exposed to the potential for offshoring over the next decade.

- The McKinsey Global Institute, in its report on the "Emerging Global La-bor Market" (MGI 2005) estimates that 9% of total U.S. employment will become potentially contestable over the next decade. This represents about 12 million jobs.

- Van Welsum and Vickery (2005), in a working paper for the OECD Informa-tion Economy Working Party, posit that about 68 separate U.S. occupations are newly at risk for offshoring, constituting 18.1% of total U.S. employment, or about 23 million jobs.

Table 4-1 translates these forecasts into implicit shares of trade in U.S. GDP (the necessary variable for the CGE models). The baseline estimate, shown in the first column of the table, is the share of jobs that are potentially tradeable in 2006, based on trade shares in national income. See Appendix 2 for the methodology involved in this translation..

Note that these are not high-end estimates. The Forrester study, for one, for reasons pointed out in Appendix 2, could be read as producing a much higher number for "potentially offshorable" jobs; Kierkegard (2004), replicating the For-rester methodology, came up with a figure of 44% of all U.S. occupations (over 50 million jobs) as newly contestable due to offshoring. These estimates actually constitute a fairly consistent mode of forecasts for the reach of offshoring over the next decade.

The results from various scenarios regarding the impact of international trade (including offshoring) on relative incomes are presented below.

Table 4-2 presents results from plugging these forecasts into the Krugman model.[25] Using the high-end forecast, from Jensen and Kletzer (2004), the Krug-man model predicts that trade could raise relative wages in 2017 by over 25%. The

TABLE 4-1. Jobs currently offshorable and forecasts for the coming decade

Current	Offshorable jobs (thousands) 14,500	Trade share 14.2%	LDC trade share 4.9%
Forecast for newly offshorable jobs by:	*(New) offshorable jobs (thousands)*	*Implied trade share*	*Implied LDC share*
Forrester Research	20,000	29.8%	10.9%
Bardhan and Kroll (2004)	14,850	25.4%	9.3%
Kletzer and Jensen (2005)	36,800	44.4%	16.2%
McKinsey Global Institute (2005)	12,029	22.9%	8.4%
Van Welsum and Vickery (2005)	18,100	28.2%	10.3%
Blinder (2006)	21,275	30.9%	11.3%
Average	20,509	30.2%	11.0%

Source: Author's calculation as described in Appendix 2.

TABLE 4-2. Offshoring's possible wage impact

	Ratio	B.A. or above	Less than B.A.
High (Jensen/Kletzer)	25.0%	10.0%	-15.0%
Low (MGI)	12.0%	5.0%	-7.0%
Blinder	17.0%	6.9%	-10.1%
Average	16.0%	6.6%	-9.4%

Source: Author's analysis using projections described in text.

low-end estimate, from MGI (2004), yields an impact of almost 12%. Simply put, this means that offshoring could lead to a rise in *relative* wages of college graduates of 12-25%. This is an amount equal to (roughly) 50-100% of the *total* increase in inequality in wage incomes of workers with and without a four-year college degree between 1979 and 2006. Offshoring, in short, has the potential to wedge apart incomes to a huge degree in a very short time.

Table 4-2 also translates these relative income results into absolute values and finds that the average of offshoring forecasts implies an increase of 8% and a decline of 9% in the wages of workers with and without a college degree, respectively. To put this in historical perspective, average hourly earnings for workers without a college degree rose by just 2.2% between 1979 and 2003. (Literally all of that growth occurred in the late 1990s.) The implied loss due to offshoring would push earnings for this group back below 1979 levels, totally undoing the wage increases these workers managed to claim over the past 30 years.

Is this really what offshoring will look like?

There are a number of reasons to reject the outcome of this (admittedly speculative) exercise. The most common rejection concerns the *types* of jobs at risk from service-sector offshoring. Many in the offshoring debate have take as a given that it is high-wage jobs that are most threatened by service-sector offshoring (Blinder, for example, takes this position).

It is, however, far from clear why the United States would all of the sudden begin importing high-wage work from poor countries just because new avenues for trade are opened. All empirical studies conducted so far on the pattern of U.S. exports and imports shows that the United States exports professional- and capital-intensive goods and imports labor-intensive goods. The economic logic of comparative advantage does not really distinguish between apparel or call-center operations, so it's unclear why the *pattern* of jobs affected by the simple introduction of new *opportunities* to trade would be different than the pattern that has characterized trade flows so far.

If, however, the United States for some reason begins importing professional- and capital-intensive work, the impact for its economy would be profound. In fact, offshoring accompanied by the wholesale reversal of what has been the comparative advantage of the United States, that is, the importing of professional- and/or capital-intensive work, holds the possibility for *aggregate* income losses to the U.S. economy, making the nation *as a whole* poorer. Paul Samuelson (2004) has put forth the most forceful (and famous) argument of this possibility, and Brad Delong (2004) has followed up. These authors emphasize different sides of the same coin. DeLong stresses the reversal of the inequality-generating aspect of globalization if offshoring leads to a comparative advantage reversal, while Samuelson stresses the aggregate income losses. In essence, both are describing a scenario that unwinds the process that is the focus of this book: trade leading to aggregate gains but distributional losses for most.

Samuelson grounds this comparative advantage reversal in the rapid growth of productivity among U.S. trading partners. If this productivity growth is biased toward sectors that were once American exporting strengths, then falling terms of trade will lead to aggregate income losses for the United States. Samuelson's article has been criticized on the grounds that it is describing not offshoring but rather well-known results from classical trade theory about export-sector biased growth in trading partners.

This critique is true enough, but surely Samuelson thought it was a given that offshoring of state-of-the-art capital and technology by U.S. multinationals lay behind rapid productivity growth in American trading partners. Ruffin and Jones (2006) make the point more explicitly and replicate the gist of the Samuelson results: export-sector technology transferred by the United States to its trading partners will indeed result in a loss for the U.S. terms of trade.

The DeLong/Samuelson view is far from implausible, and if offshoring makes the United States relatively less education- and/or capital-abundant relative to its low-wage trading partners, then the limits of the terms of trade reversal sketched out by Samuelson imply an income loss of roughly $70-80 billion for the United States. This isn't catastrophic (the U.S. economy grows by roughly three to four times this amount in a given year), but it does point out that the scenarios sketched out in this chapter can be thought of as the best-case scenario for the U.S. economy as a whole arising from the realization of offshoring forecasts.

Angst over offshoring is utterly rational. If the practice leads to a reversal of U.S. comparative advantage, non-trivial amounts of aggregate income will be lost. And if it is just more of the same kind of trade that we've seen in past decades, it will provide a powerful leveling force on global wages, one that will not work to American workers' advantage.

CHAPTER 5

Benchmarking the costs of globalization

The trade and wages literature, while exhaustive, has generally not described its findings in a manner readily understandable to policy makers or the wider public. The most common metric in the debate expresses the influence of trade as a share of the total growth in inequality over a given time period. As noted before, this benchmark has provided fodder for those who minimize globalization's impact on American workers. The reason is simple: the increase in American inequality over the past 30-odd years has been so extraordinary that *anything* compared to it might look trivial. But noting that trade explains less than a majority of the total increase in inequality is a debater's point meant not to inform but to choke off debate.

When expressed in more-recognizable terms such as: dollars per worker or dollars per household, or compared to other benchmarks that loom large in public debates about economics, the costs of globalization can be illuminated. This chapter provides such measures.

How much inequality, and how much of it?

The growth in the gap between wages of workers with and without college degrees over the last 30 years was detailed in Chapter 3. Wages for workers without a four-year degree have barely budged since 1979, rising 0.4%, while wages for workers with at least a four-year degree have risen 24.4%. The result is a 24% increase in the relative wage of workers with a degree. This gap has grown even when other characteristics besides education (race, age, sex, region of residence, marital status) are controlled for.

This chapter largely ignores the "share of total inequality" rubric as a method for understanding globalization's importance. Instead, it tries to translate the costs of globalization into simple dollar amounts, and then compares those totals to other economic costs facing U.S. households. Readers can then weigh for themselves whether the costs are significant or not.

How much in dollars?

Is globalization's impact large or small? The answer may depend on whether you think that, say, a thousand dollars a year is a little or a lot of money. The best way to make an assessment is to express the costs of globalization for Americans af-

TABLE 5-1. Benchmarking the costs of globalization for affected families

	Costs for affected workers	Costs for households
1. Globalization's costs for workers on the losing end	$1,420	$2,560
2. Closing 75-year funding gap in Social Security	$610	$1,070
3. Financing Bush tax cuts with spending cuts	.	$1,510
4. Average federal income tax paid by middle-income households	.	$1,550
5. Average out-of-pocket spending on health care (including premiums)	$1,590	$2,783
6. Savings for a four-year college education, starting in 2007	.	$1,060
7. Burden of rising gas and fuel oil prices since 2002		$1,510
8. Current funding for Trade Adjustment Assistance	$11	.
9. Gains to workers with a four-year degree from globalization	$2,285	.

Source: Author's analysis.

fected adversely by it in dollar terms, rather than as a percentage change in this or that relative wage or as a share of some other large number.

Table 5-1 provides the simple dollar figures for what globalization has cost American workers without a four-year college degree and compares how these costs stack up to some other economic costs that are frequently discussed in public debate. The table also considers the impact on two representative earners/households. The first is a single full-time worker who earns the median wage. The second is a household consisting of two median wage earners who work a combined 3,600 hours a year (this is the average hours worked per year for married couples age 25-54 with children).

The first row uses the mid-estimate from the computable general equilibrium model from Chapter 3, which indicated a 4.8% wage loss for workers without a degree. For a full-time median-wage earner in 2006, this translates into an annual earnings loss of $1,420. For a household with two earners, the mid-estimate of their losses is $2,560.

It bears repeating that this loss to workers and households is *permanent* and repeats year after year. Global integration cost affected workers at least $1,000 in 2006 and presumably (assuming no decline in trade flows) cost them at least this much again in 2007 and so on. **Figure 5-A** shows the average annual estimates for what trade flows have cost affected workers over time since 1973, when the U.S. economy was for all intents and purposes closed to trade with less-developed coun-

FIGURE 5-A. Annual earnings for full-time, median-wage earner, 1973-2006

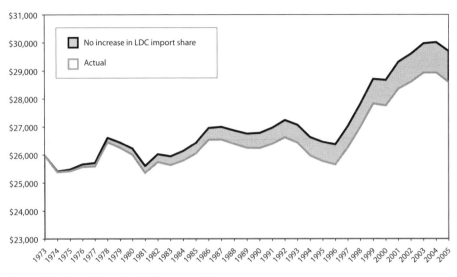

Source: Author's calculations using the Krguman model.

tries. The cumulative loss between then and 2006 for a full-time worker who made the median wage each year would have exceeded $17,000 by 2006. By any serious reckoning, this is real money.

How much compared to what?

Succeeding rows of Table 5-1 benchmark the costs of globalization to a number of other economic costs facing American households. The first such benchmark is the cost of insuring 75-year actuarial solvency of the U.S. Social Security system strictly through an immediate across-the-board increase in the payroll tax rate.[26] This 75-year shortfall is frequently characterized as a sword of Damocles hanging above the heads of American families. Yet the costs of globalization exceed the costs of closing the long-run Social Security financing gap by an order of 2 to 1.

There is an irony in the use of the Social Security shortfall as a comparison because the single most important reason for the deterioration of Social Security's long-term financing since the reforms introduced in 1983 is the rapid growth in wage inequality since that year.[27] In other words, the modest but inflated cost of closing the 75-year financing gap today is in part the *result* of globalization.

Another useful benchmark compares the cost of globalization for an affected worker to the cost to paying for the Bush administration tax cuts with an across-the-board cut in government spending. Jason Furman and William Gale (2007) have documented these costs exhaustively and transparently, and the $1,510 figure used in the table is their number for households in the middle income quintile. Most people would consider this a large hit against these households, yet the costs of globalization exceed them.

It's worth noting here that, if there is a single issue that unites the entire center-left coalition in American politics, it is opposition to financing the Bush tax cuts with spending cuts, opposition that rests in large part on the distributional un-fairness of such a policy. A wide-ranging study of the Bush tax cuts by Furman (2006) noted that the strategy of paying for the Bush tax cuts with across-the-board reductions in government spending could achieve small economy-wide efficiency gains—roughly 0.03% extra GDP growth annually for 20 years. Furman then went on to argue that achieving these efficiency gains would not justify the distributional unfairness of financing the tax cuts with spending cuts. Apply this argument to globalization. Small efficiency gains at the cost of substantial upward redistribution *is exactly the effect of globalization on the U.S. economy*. Yet globalization stands as perhaps the most politically fractious issue for the center-left coalition.

Row 4 provides the benchmark of *all* federal income taxes paid by families in the middle income quintile. The costs of globalization to affected workers exceeds their federal income tax bill (roughly $1,600 for our typical household). If this dollar amount for taxes seems low, it needs to be noted that the majority of American households pay more in federal payroll taxes (to support Social Security and Medicare) than they do in federal income taxes. Further, for a middle-income family, the burden of state income taxes, sales taxes, and excise taxes are large relative to the federal income tax burden. In short, the federal income tax is still relatively progressive (though less so than it was before the Bush administration tax cuts). That said, few middle-class Americans would characterize their federal income tax bill as "small."

Row 5 shows an economic benchmark that looms large in the public debate: per capita out-of-pocket spending on health care, including individual contributions for health insurance premiums.

These costs, $1,590 per worker in 2006, either exceed or rival those of globalization, and they have sparked public anxiety and intense policy discussions over the role of health care and its costs for American living standards. This is a case where the elite conventional wisdom has it right: rising health care costs are a substantial burden. Yet the costs of globalization rivaled those for out-of-pocket medical expenditures for the majority of American households in 2006.

Row 6 shows the cost of a four-year college degree, calculated assuming that a family begins saving annually with the birth of a child and has to pay a lump-sum for a degree at a public university when the child turns 18. The annual total, $1,060, is serious money for middle-income families, but it is still less than the amount globalization is siphoning away. And since this is the amount that a worker will have to pay to help insure that his or her child will not wind up in the same boat, it's a little bit ironic.[28]

Row 7 compares the costs of globalization to the cost of rising gas and fuel oil prices for a middle-income family. Since 2002, the price of gasoline and fuel oil has risen by over 140%. Assuming that this family didn't cut its consumption in response to the price rise, the extra it must pay is $1,510 by 2008. And still, the much more hidden costs of globalization are greater.

Row 8 shows the costs of globalization relative to the trade adjustment assistance (TAA) program, a federal program that aids workers displaced by trade and which is often pointed to as constituting fair compensation for the damage done American workers by trade. In 2006, funding for this program was roughly $860 million, representing about 1/500th of the amount of income that is taken from workers on the losing end of globalization.

Recently, a number of commentators have suggested supplements to TAA, usually in the form of "wage insurance," a federal guarantee to pay some portion of the difference between a worker's pre- and post-displacement wage for a limited time. Various wage-insurance proposals could add anywhere between $2 billion and $10 billion to the overall price tag, but these increases would still leave more than 90% of the costs of globalization completely uncompensated for in terms of government transfers.

The last row shows the average gain accruing to workers with a four-year degree from the United States integration into the global market. While integration of the rich United States and poorer global economy harms *most* American workers, it remains true that *winnings* exceed *losses* as a result of this integration. This exercise is useful for a number of reasons. First, it reminds readers that globalization should indeed be expected to deliver net national gains. Second, the ratio of winnings to losses is a key parameter in determining how difficult the political task of compensation is going to be. The ratios in this row provide an answer to the common question, why is globalization such a fractious issue in American politics? After all, the classic (and correct) view about global integration's impact on the American economy argues that, while it creates both winners and losers, winnings are greater than losses, so the winners can fully compensate the losers and still come out ahead.

It turns out, however, that a single number determines whether or not globalization will be a political problem in the real world: the ratio of winnings to losses.

Before turning to the real-world numbers, let's take two examples to illustrate this point. In case one, globalization results in equal numbers of winners and losers. Winners' incomes rise by $1,000 and losers' incomes fall by $1. Winners could give up $1 (or 0.1% of their winnings) to hold the losers harmless and still remain much better off than before. In case two, however, globalization results again in equal numbers of winners and losers, and winners' incomes again rise by $1,000, but now losers' incomes fall by $999. Full compensation in this case requires winners forking over 99.9% of their entire gain to hold losers harmless. Failure to do so, moreover, leaves losers in a deep hole.

Too often, the American debate over globalization has implicitly characterized it roughly conforming to case one: huge aggregate benefits and rather small costs. Further, the costs are generally characterized as falling on a small portion of the American workforce—blue-collar manufacturing workers. Even well-known trade experts occasionally frame the problem as closer to case one. Matthew Slaughter, former member of the Bush administration's Council of Economic Advisors, and Kenneth Scheve, a political science professor at Yale University, argue in *Foreign Affairs* magazine for a truly ambitious policy proposal to aid the losers from globalization: zero out the payroll tax for all workers earning less than the median wage. Slaughter and Scheve seem unconcerned that this plan would hamstring the finances of Social Security, but, this aspect aside, they are talking serious money— roughly $260 billion would essentially be transferred to those at the median point of the income distribution and below.

Slaughter and Scheve move on to argue that the gains from trade are so huge that this reform should be relatively easy to accomplish politically. In support of this contention, they cite a deeply flawed study by the Peterson Institute of International Economics that argues that moving from today's U.S. trade policy of less than 2% average tariffs to a trade policy with zero tariffs would generate $500 billion for the U.S. economy. Appendix 4 takes on that claim (and Bivens 2007a, 2007b, 2007c provides a full accounting of what's wrong with the Peterson study), but suffice it to say that this $500 billion will not be seen anytime soon.

Sadly, both for political peace as well as for the living standards of American workers left behind by globalization, we're a lot closer to case two: small national benefits, but substantial losses that reach a huge swath (likely the majority) of the U.S. workforce. The losses have been well-documented so far in this chapter—more than $1,000 annually for workers without a four-year college degree. The last row of the table shows the gross gains to those with a four-year degree from global integration: $2,285. Given that workers without a degree greatly outnumber those with a degree, these numbers imply that fully compensating the former group would require dipping pretty deeply into the winners' gains. Essentially, roughly 90% of the gross winnings of those benefiting from globalization would have to be redistributed to hold the losing group harmless.

This redistribution is the first-best response to the pressures globalization puts on American workers. However, given the substantial gap between losses and national gains, the politics will not be easy, and pretending that they are represents either a fundamental misunderstanding of the economics of globalization or else a political dodge to argue against fundamental changes in the globalization status quo.

Conclusion: Which is the right benchmark?

The rapidly diverging fortunes of Americans at different income levels have made it impossible to speak confidently about what is good or bad for the American economy as a whole. Simply speaking, there is no one American economy but multitudes. Some are enjoying almost unbelievable prosperity. Others (ones containing far more actual people) are struggling to match the steady rise in living standards that seemed promised by the first 30 years following World War II.

Globalization has made a significant contribution to this fracturing of American economic interests, and it illustrates most plainly the new fact that what is good for one American economy may not be good for others. Given this, choosing the proper benchmark for evaluating the outcomes of globalization in the American economy then becomes firmly a matter of politics, not technical economics. In the globalization debate, many economists have tried to claim that this is not the case, and that adherence to economic logic requires favoring the net national gains of globalization even at the expense of large gross losses to those already relatively worse-off.

Workers harmed by globalization have been profoundly ill-served by economists in the American debate over globalization. The utterly rational fears of American workers, grounded firmly in the foundational material of economic textbooks, are overlooked by those more concerned with raising average rather than typical incomes. When forced to admit that globalization does indeed come with some costs, economists advocating the globalization status quo often minimize the costs. This stance is mean politics and bad economics.

Future rounds of the globalization debate need to offer solutions that match the scale of the costs globalization has inflicted and can be expected to inflict in the future. How to move the debate in that direction is the subject of next chapter.

Enemies or friends?
The economics textbook and an egalitarian response to globalization

There is very little in the economics textbook that demands support of globalization as currently practiced. This fact needs to become better known.

The predictable result of a rich U.S. economy integrating with a poorer global economy is net national gains but with large gross wins and losses within each economy. For the United States, the winnings go to workers with the skills, capital, and credentials to keep them insulated from the global labor market. Losses are borne by the U.S. workers (a majority) that are disproportionately represented in sectors most exposed to import competition. And it's not just workers directly displaced by imports who are damaged: it's all workers economy-wide who have similar education and skills.

Too often the answer to these losses is, "well, then Americans need to get educated."

Over 70% of the American workforce lacks a four-year college degree. Doesn't it seem odd to blame the outcome of an economic trend that has predictably harmed the majority of the American workforce on a failure of personal initiative?

Further, the factor that allows more educated and credentialed workers in the United States to escape damage from global integration has nothing to do with their own personal productivity or initiative. Rather, it's just the arbitrary fact that they were born in a capital-rich country. This capital abundance means that U.S. imports will be labor-intensive and thus put no pressure on their own incomes. But highly skilled and credentialed workers in labor-abundant countries, who are individually every bit as able and productive as their American counterparts, can just as easily suffer from global integration as their American counterparts have benefited.[29] In short, there is little reason for globalization's winners to be smug: the pattern for losses and winnings is essentially arbitrary with respect to an individual worker's characteristics.

When good economists go bad

While many policy makers either genuinely do not understand what economics teaches about globalization or do not understand that national income does not equal national welfare, there is a large subclass of smart, progressive policy makers and economists who engage in fierce defense of the globalization *status quo*. It's widespread enough a phenomena to merit an extended aside here.

This group knows all too well that trade is (or at least could be) bad for the broad working class in the United States, yet they embrace trade agreements like NAFTA and the World Trade Organization in the name of expanding the economic possibilities facing workers in the world's poor countries, who benefit from easy access to the U.S. market for their exports.

This is a real and ethical concern. It's also a politically powerful argument. But this concern, however real, needs to be the beginning, not the end, of a conversation.

The first thing to note about this argument is how divorced it is from what the economics textbook actually teaches about the benefits of trade. The vast majority of the textbook gains from trade stem not from countries' ability to *export* to other countries, but from their access to cheaper *imports*. Paul Krugman put it best:

> Even more fundamentally, we should be able to teach students that imports, not exports, are the purpose of trade. That is, what a country gains from trade is the ability to import things it wants. Exports are not an objective in and of themselves: the need to export is a burden that a country must bear because its import suppliers are crass enough to demand payment. (Krugman 1996.]

Essentially, the textbook teaches that any country can reap much of the benefits of trade unilaterally. Evidence of this can be found in the World Bank's examination of the effect of trade liberalization on developing countries in its 2002 report, *Global Economic Prospects and Developing Countries*. The protected agricultural markets of rich countries are often cited as prime impediments to developing country growth. Yet the World Bank (2002) estimates the gains to removing their own agricultural protections would yield developing countries benefits four times greater than the removal of barriers to this trade in rich countries. For all kinds of trade, the removal of their own barriers by developing countries yields benefits more than twice as large as the removal of barriers to rich countries.

Dropping textbook purism

The economics textbook tells us that the real gains from trade to developing countries lies in their ability to import cheap goods that they can't produce efficiently themselves (cars, trucks, airplanes, machine tools, etc.). But there are many reasons to believe that access to the U.S. consumer market may actually be more valuable to developing countries than one would judge from just reading the textbook. In fact, economists have found enormously interesting (and admittedly sometimes ambiguous) things about the effects of globalization on growth.

The most persuasive of these theories concerns the link between trade, technology, and economic growth: globalization, by leading to increased technology transfer between countries, allows developing countries to move more rapidly to the First World technology frontier. As technological change is a primary driver of economic growth, this transfer could lead to sustained growth as developing countries catch up to the industrial countries.

A key ingredient for this technology transfer and catch-up is exposure to competition from selling in the markets of the globe's industrial core. Competing for segments of the United States market has led to a more efficient economy in China and Mexico and some other major U.S. trading partners and played a huge role in the economic development of Japan, South Korea, and Taiwan.

None of this, however, demands allegiance to the globalization *status quo*. The mistaken premise that leads one from recognizing the value of U.S. market access to an uncritical acceptance of today's version of globalization is that this access is provided at low cost by the current global trading regime. From this premise, tampering with the *status quo* is a move toward reducing access or making it more expensive. But such is not the case.

Knowing its value, the United States has used access to its consumer market as a powerful lever to compel developing country governments to adopt a range of policy preferences that they would likely not adopt on their own. Under this regime, the cost of access to the U.S. market imposed by the globalization status quo is restricted "policy space" for developing countries.

The North American Free Trade Agreement is a case study in this dynamic. American barriers to Mexican imports were already low by 1993, and so NAFTA in this regard promised little marginal benefit to Mexican exporters. Instead, what NAFTA did offer was a promise that this access could be insured in perpetuity if the Mexican government adopted a range of policies amenable to the corporate class in each country. Conveniently, many of these policies were generally favored by a neoliberal, technocratic Mexican government that would have found them hard to sell on their own merits but found them more convincing when tied to the promise that NAFTA would benefit the wider Mexican economy by giving Mexican exports a boost.

The contingent policy provisions were essentially a range of investor protections, many of them wholly unrelated to trade. Some of the most controversial provide protections against government expropriations. While many might think that guarding against government seizure of private assets is a decidedly non-radical step, market fundamentalists and multinationals have engaged in a fierce campaign to define expropriation as essentially any government policy that reduces a firm's profitability. Surely, giving chemical companies the right to sue governments for compensation when their profits are reduced by environmental regulation is not what most people think of as free trade, yet this is how NAFTA's provisions have been interpreted by many multinationals.

The formation of the World Trade Organization from the old General Agreement on Tariffs and Trade (GATT) followed NAFTA's lead in wringing odd, non-trade-related policy concessions from developing nations as a price of admission to the markets of the industrial countries.

Of course, the value of access to the U.S. market is severely degraded if the cost of having it is a radical restriction of policy autonomy. Occasionally defenders of the neoliberal policy program that is the intellectual foundation for today's globalization *status quo* argue that the policies foisted upon poorer signatories of the treaties governing global trade are actually beneficial to their own growth. In fact, one can make the case that during the neoliberal heyday of the mid-1980s to mid-1990s the policy restrictions were actually a feature, not a bug, of the global trading regime from the perspective of these neoliberal policy makers.

The evidence pointing to the growth-enhancing properties of neoliberal economic policies pushed on the world's poor by the globalization *status quo*, however, is sorely lacking. It cannot be an accident that the list of countries that have used (or are using) U.S. market access as a key tool for economic development either made their developmental leap before the tight strictures of today's rules governing globalization fell into place (Japan), received dispensation from many of the strictures on geopolitical grounds (South Korea and Taiwan), or just flat ignored most of them (China and India).

Indeed, the list of developing nations that have managed to make the leap to the middle-income strata or are posting impressive growth rates through the 1990s and 2000s correlates shockingly well with those that are in greatest contravention of the policy preferences enshrined in today's global trading system. India, China, and Vietnam, for example, are often held up as nations benefiting from opening up to world trade. Yet each of them carefully managed and protected certain sectors of their economy, engaged in intelligently directed industrial policy initiatives, and had often achieved impressive growth rates *before* joining the WTO or engaging in deregulation of international trade. As Chang (2002) has persuasively argued, economic history makes a convincing case that making access to the U.S. market contingent upon abandoning the tools of activist trade and industrial policies for their own economies is all but guaranteed to hamstring growth in the world's poorest countries.

What, then, is a progressive trade policy?

The interests of workers in America and abroad can conflict at times, but this is no reason for despair among those concerned about the welfare of workers in both rich and poor countries, nor is it a reason to accede the high ground of morality or economic logic to the *status quo*.

There is a simple way to thread the needle between the interests of workers at home and abroad: making access to the U.S. market contingent not on investor protections or other egregious restrictions on policy space, but on the adoption and vigorous enforcement of the core labor standards identified by the International Labor Organization (ILO) as essential in protecting workers' rights.

These core labor standards essentially guarantee the right of association and collective bargaining, the right to freedom from labor market discrimination, and prohibition of forced labor or exploitative child labor. While not guaranteeing economic outcomes (such as imposing an international minimum wage), the labor standards would buttress the bargaining power of workers globally, thereby providing a legitimacy to global competition and quite possibly leading to absolute improvements in living standards.

Aidt and Tzannatos (2002) offer qualified evidence that freedom of association and collective bargaining rights can be a useful tool in aiding productivity growth. The OECD (1996) offers similarly qualified evidence that economic performance in nations that have undertaken significant labor standards reform (expanding workers' rights) see higher GDP growth rates post-reform. Rodrik (1998) and Palley (2001) have assembled powerful evidence that political freedoms (broadly defined by Rodrik and specifically identified with labor standards by Palley) are correlated with wage growth, even after controlling for productivity.

The most common argument against making labor standards a condition for market access—that it is just disguised protectionism—finds little support in the data. The OECD (1996) study found no correlation between adoption and enforcement of these standards on a country's international trade or investment performance.

A trade regime founded on workers' rights would fully recognize the right of workers in poor countries to compete on the basis of low wages, but it would prohibit competition based on the deprivation of workers' basic rights. Given that the bias of the evidence so far is that greater political freedoms correlate with better economic performance, a strong argument can be made that a global trading regime based on labor standards above all would solve a possible coordination problem in not allowing any single country to gain competitive trade advantages by suppressing workers' rights.

It should be noted that the United States has been found wanting by the ILO on the basis of its own noncompliance with meaningful enforcement of some of the core labor standards (especially with regard to prison labor and the freedom of association). The U.S. record provides perfectly reasonable cover for developing countries that want to provide protection for their own markets from U.S. goods for a time.

Enforcement of core labor standards, based on cross-border labor solidarity, should *replace*, not just *augment*, all the corporate clutter that constitutes the current price of admission to today's global trading regime.

After insuring the basic rights of workers, the United States and the other industrial powers that run the institutions governing globalization should back off and let developing countries experiment with whatever policies they think will be effective and sustainable for their own economies. Until the policy-making autonomy of developing countries is insured, the benefits they can gain from the current terms that condition access to the U.S. market will be minuscule at best and negative at worst. Further, and, most important, swapping labor standards for the menu of corporate preferences as the key to U.S. market access will actually be a move toward a *more liberal* trading regime, and at the same time provide legitimacy to the global trading system. This swap is clearly win-win from the perspective of workers both in the United States and its poorer trading partners.

To date, the economic elites in the United States and around the world have championed a global trading system that provides huge benefits to themselves while radically reducing the economic possibilities of the world's poor. When this integration predictably damaged the broad working and middle class in the United States along the way, these same elites promote this status quo as necessary for protecting the global poor. And why would anybody want to impede that worthy goal?

Even if it were true that the beneficiaries of the contemporary rules governing globalization were the very wealthy and the poorest of the poor (wouldn't that make an interesting economic model), indifference about significant damage being inflicted on the American middle class would be callous and wrong. But it's not the case, and protecting the world's poor is simply not a goal or outcome of the rules of the game governing globalization today.

What to do domestically

A global trading regime that rests on a foundation of respect for workers' rights is rightly a key goal for progressives. Yet it is far too small a policy counterweight to the pressures globalization has brought and will continue to bring to bear on American living standards.

Even if the basic rights of workers in the world's poorest countries are secured, there will still remain hundreds of millions willing to labor at much lower wage rates than Americans, and pressure on American wages will result. In short, the real problems regarding globalization and its impact on American workers does not reside in the rules of the game governing this integration, but simply in the fact that this integration is happening on any terms at all.

Given that trade policy does not provide a long enough lever to solve the problem, it seems that a new strategy is needed. This new strategy would emphasize a core progressive principle: *your economic lot in life is not wholly of your own making.*

The damage inflicted by the integration of the United States into the global economy requires compensation. Targeted programs to help those most directly and catastrophically affected by trade—programs like Trade Adjustment Assistance—are a step in that direction today, but the funding for these programs (as detailed in Chapter 5 for TAA) does not come anywhere close to the costs of globalization for affected workers.

Just as important as the gap between the scale of damage and remedy is chronology. Workers should be cajoled into accepting the added risk of trade *after* they've been assured of a political commitment to egalitarian policies to lean against the damage of globalization, and not before.

While it is surely true that the causes of inequality needn't match up to solutions, it does not then follow that the causes of inequality are irrelevant to political debate. When we recognize that a significant portion of inequality is driven by evolving circumstances that arbitrarily change the rewards to different workers, and when we acknowledge that these changes have benefited relatively few at the expense of the many, then an appeal to provide compensation for these changes, based on solidarity and simple fairness, holds a much better chance of working.

Judging by the equanimity with which Americans have historically accepted inequality, it seems that we view inequality as largely representing the just rewards to ability and effort. As regards globalization, because the debate so far has stressed the downsides of globalization only for those workers who are directly displaced by trade, the vast majority of American workers think that it has either not affected their working lives or, if it has, it has only made many things they buy cheaper. It may be too bad for those manufacturing workers in the Rust Belt, but whose problem is that?

Global integration is everyone's issue and everyone's problem. Rising inequality and wage pressures on large swathes of the workforce are not the rewards and punishment for differential talent and effort. Rather, they are the result of the rules of the economic game changing around the players, in ways they never voted for.

APPENDIX 1

Technical appendices

Appendix 1A: HOT spinoffs

Stolper-Samuelson theorem (SST)

The punchline of the SST is that tariff protection raises the return to a nation's scarce factor and tariff cutting (symmetrically) reduces it. This result is driven by the response of goods prices to a tariff cut (or cuts in other trade costs). The original SST relied on a set of rather strict assumptions: identical production technology available across nations and identical demand preferences across economies. Over time, it has been shown to be generalizable along many dimensions (see Ethier (1997) for more on this).

Roughly following Deardorff (1994), the logic of the SST runs as follows.

A tariff cut reduces the price of imported goods by the full amount of the tariff. The decrease in the price of imports will be matched by an equal fall in the price of domestically made goods that compete with imports. Essentially, domestic producers lose the competitive space provided by the tariff that allowed them to keep domestic prices high on their import-competing goods. As prices for import-competing goods fall, more of the economy's resources shift away from this sector and toward the export sector as producing import-competing goods now has become less profitable.

This resource shift reduces demand for the factor used intensively in the import-competing industry. That is, as (say) a cut in steel tariffs makes domestic steel production less profitable, steel producers will shed resources to the rest of the economy in proportions that "look" like the resources it already uses. If producing steel is a labor-intensive activity, this means decreasing production in the domestic steel industry reduces the demand for labor.

How do we know for sure that a tariff cut will always lead to a decline in the demand for a country's scarce factor? Remember the HOT demonstrated that import-competing goods, by dint of a nation's endowment, always make intensive use of the nation's scarce factor.

As producers exit the import-competing sector competition (which ensures that output prices equal the cost of inputs), this guarantees that the *average* prices for all factors employed there must fall (relatively) by the same amount as the fall in the price of the import-competing good (that is, by the amount of the tariff cut).

If the scarce factor is not the only factor employed in the import-competing sector the decline in *average* factor prices in this sector means that its own price must fall *relative to this average, and hence relative to the price of the import-competing good*. That is, we know that the average reduction in factor prices in the import-competing sectors is, say, 10%, but we also know that *only the scarce factor loses out due to tariff cutting*. Given this, the entire decline in the price of the import-competing goods must be wrung out of returns to the scarce factor.

If, say, labor accounts for 70% of the final price of a good, and we know the price of this good has fallen by 10% and that the entirety of this 10% fall must come out of the return to labor, this means labor costs must fall by at least 10% divided by 70%, or 14% (actually, more than this, since the other input into production, professional labor is actually rising in price). Hence, we know that the fall in wages must be greater than the price decline of imports (and import-competing goods), so labor loses in absolute (price-adjusted) terms in this instance.

The Rybcynski theorem (RT)

The most famous prediction of the RT is actually not the one identified in the body of the text; rather, it is a prediction that an increase in the supply of one productive factor (say labor) will lead to an increase in the production of the good that intensively uses this factor and a decrease in the sector that does not, as long as the ratio of commodity prices (the *terms of trade*) remain constant.

Essentially, this says that a large increase in one factor of production (say labor) does not have to impact relative factor returns within a country whose commodity prices are determined on global markets—the factor inflow will be seamlessly absorbed by shifting production toward the sector that intensively uses it. The assumption on unchanging terms of trade is the important bit here; if an economy becomes so integrated with the rest of the world that domestic prices exactly mirror global ones, then, and only then, relative factor supplies are irrelevant to factor returns.

The logic of this would argue that an enormous inflow of immigration of labor into a given nation would have no effect on wages if the nation was already sufficiently integrated into the global economy. It has been suggested that Rybczynski effects explain some of the apparent lack of effect of large-scale immigration from Mexico into the United States (Card 2005). More forcefully, it has been argued that Israel (a small country that may well have little ability to make domestic prices diverge from global ones) has absorbed even much larger proportional inflows of labor with very little in the way of measurable wage effects during the 1980s and 1990s (Gandal et al. 1999).

When the terms of trade are not assumed fixed, then the RT becomes relevant to the question of what happens when the global labor pool increases—the question addressed earlier in the main body of this chapter.

The factor price equalization theorem (FPET)

The FPET, as noted before, requires rather heroic assumptions to hold literally true. Essentially, these assumptions are that each nation has identical technology available to it, prices for goods in any given country are totally determined by global markets (and unaffected by domestic influences), and production is not specialized—each country makes a bit of everything. Given these (rather stringent) assumptions, the logic of the FPET runs as follows.

First, arbitrage made possible by trade equates commodity prices across countries. That is, absent barriers to trade, goods prices everywhere will equalize. Second, because technology is identical across countries, there is a unique relationship between commodity prices, factor ratios, and factor prices. This means that, given commodity prices, each nation will chose the exact same technology, defined as the ratio of factor inputs (the most efficient ratio) for production. Third, since each country uses the same ratio of factor inputs in production, and since the price of commodities is equal across nations, the *ratio* of rents to wages is equal across nations.

Lastly, the *absolute* price of any factor is the product of its productivity in generating output and the price of output. Identical technology ensures that factor productivities are identical across nations, and arbitrage ensures that output prices are equalized. Hence, *absolute*, not just *relative*, factor prices will equalize across nations. A key assumption here again is that nations are not *completely* specialized in either good; the unique relationship between commodity prices and factor prices only holds globally if each nation produces output in each industry.

This last bit (at least) makes intuitive sense: if there are absolutely no jobs producing apparel in the United States, for example, then there is no way that future declines in the price of importing apparel production from China or Mexico can threaten the demand for U.S. labor (already zero) in these sectors.

Appendix 1B: Estimating techniques (FCA, PPR, CGE)

Factor content analysis (FCA)

The method of factor contents is fairly straightforward. Assuming that there are only two goods (X and Y) to measure the amount of skilled labor "embodied" in trade flows simply multiply the ratio of the trade balance (D) in good X by the skilled-labor (S) input coefficient associated with the domestic production of X. Add to this the equivalent calculation for good Y to obtain the following expression for the impact of trade on the implicit labor supply of S.

(1) $\Delta S = S_x \Delta D_x + S_y \Delta D_y$

Here, D is the difference between domestic production (Q) and domestic consumption (C) of each good (or the sectoral trade deficit). Given the assumption that the entire supply of S is exhausted in the production of X and Y, the proportional change in the implicit labor supply of S driven by trade flows can be derived as follows, with a "hat" over a variable denoting proportional changes:

(2) $\hat{S} = s_x \hat{D}_x + (1 - s_x) \hat{D}_y$

Here, s is the share of all skilled labor engaged in the production of good X. This expression thus gives the proportional change in the implicit labor supply of skilled workers stemming from trade flows.

To obtain the implicit labor supply of less-skilled labor L, embodied in trade flows, one repeats the exercise for L. The key parameters for translating trade flows into labor market outcomes are shown clearly here: the trade deficit/surplus in each industry (D) and the relative labor intensity of production (S or L) in each industry.

The results from the factor content analysis can be combined with data on economy-wide educational shares of employment to back out the implicit labor supply and wage impacts stemming from the factor proportions impact of trade. The relationship between proportional changes in relative wages (w) and labor supplies of skilled (S) and less-skilled (L) labor can be summed up:

(3) $\hat{w} = -\dfrac{\hat{S} - \hat{L}}{\sigma}$

Given that the changes in relative labor supplies have been derived previously, one just needs to divide the differences by the elasticity of substitution between skilled and less-skilled workers (σ) to obtain the implicit relative wage impact of trade flows.

Product price regressions

Product price regressions (PPR) are based on the SST theory linking changes in product prices and changes to wages and rents. In the case of the United States, the common presumption is that, for trade to exacerbate inequality, the prices of labor-intensive goods must display price declines relative to other goods. The most common form of PPRs take the form:

(4) $\hat{p}_{it} = A + LX_{it} + e_{it}$

Here p refers to prices in industry i in time period t, with a "hat" representing proportional change, L refers to the share of (less-skilled) labor in industry i in period t, and e is a random error term.

Almost all studies find a simple correlation between (less-skilled) labor intensity and product price declines (and if the computer-producing sector is removed, all studies do). As more controls are added to the equation, however, the correlation sometimes breaks down.

The most important control added to some PPR studies is a measure of total factor productivity (*tfp*). This control essentially allows one to measure the relationship between price changes *not driven by technological change* and the labor intensity of an industry. Leamer (1998) essentially argues that after controlling for *tfp* growth in an industry, the remainder of price changes can be attributed to "globalization." It must be noted that this is a pretty ironic reversal of much of the inequality literature. In much of this literature, any residual not accounted for by other influences that drive inequality are assumed to be claimed by technology. While some versions of these PPR regressions assume a 1-for-1 reduction in industry prices resulting from *tfp* growth, others use "pass-through" coefficients to parse out how much *tfp* advances reduce industry prices. Leamer (1998) examines a range of assumed pass-through coefficients to obtain a range of estimates about the impact of trade on wages, while Feenstra and Hanson (1999) estimate their pass-through coefficient econometrically.

Another important control that came to be important in later generations of the PPR studies is the inclusion of controls for changes in intermediate input prices. Intermediate inputs account for generally over half the value of final shipments in manufacturing industries, so price swings here can greatly affect regressions of final output prices.

While the first-generation of PPR studies generally regressed the *change* in industry prices on the *level* of (a given grade of) labor intensity, second-generation models expressed price changes as a function of factor cost *shares* and changes in factor prices, and these second-generation specifications are inarguably more in line with the predictions of the SST.

When the PPR regression is estimated in its "changes" form, however, if one assumes a zero-profit condition (i.e., competitive product markets), then the resulting expression is an accounting identity. Essentially, assuming competition, prices equal the sum on input costs, so once one accounts for input price changes and one (of two) factor price changes, there's no variation in value-added prices left to be explained, so the expression becomes an accounting identity.

Leamer (1998) and Krueger (1997), in recognizing this, term the outcomes of their regressions with varying assumptions regarding the *tfp* pass-through coefficient to be expressing "mandated" changes in wages that are implied by the pattern of product price changes. Krueger (1997) notes that sampling errors, measurement errors, and possible noncompetitive behavior could still introduce some error into the estimating equation. Further, Krueger (1997) chooses to not include *tfp* in the estimating equation. He argues that if *tfp* growth is uncorrelated with (share-weighted) input price growth variables, it will just add random error. If it is correlated with input shares, it will load up on these variables. The general form of the "mandated" wage expression used by Leamer (1998) and Krueger (1997) is:

(5) $\hat{p}_j + (1 - \lambda)\hat{tfp}_j = B_j \hat{\theta}_j + e_j$

In this expression, the estimated parameter B is defined as the change in factor returns (wages) that are required to keep profits zero in the face of changes in technology (*tfp*) and product prices (*p*). If one imagines that influences besides globalization are exhausted by the inclusion of the *tfp* control, then one can interpret this as the effect of globalization on wages. An alternative view would say that this represents the ceiling of globalization's effect on wages. Krueger (1997), as noted before, assumes that equals one (full pass-through of technological change into sector prices), and hence *tfp* falls out of his estimating equation. This equation (5) is what we use here in the updates to the PPR regression studies in Chapter 3.

Feenstra and Hanson (1999) take a different tack in interpreting this expression. They construct an expression of price change in an industry similar to (5), but specify terms so as to make the expression an *identity*, not a relationship to be estimated. Formally, their expression is:

(6) $\hat{p}_j + = -TFP_{jt} + (1/2)(s_{jt-1} + s_{jt})\Delta w_{jt}$

Here, the *p* represents the change (hence the "hat") in value-added prices in industry *j* in time period *t*, *w* represents a vector of "effective" factor prices (wages and returns to capital, adjusted for quality differences between industries), and *s* refers to factor cost shares in total value-added average over the most recent two time periods.

The measure of total factor productivity that they use (the dual Tornqvist) is defined as precisely the difference between the change in industry prices and the cost-share weighted change in factor prices. This makes (6) an identity.

From here, Feenstra and Hanson "endogenize" the change in prices and productivity in order to isolate the impacts of structural variables like trade (which they define as outsourcing, or the share of intermediate inputs into production that are imported) and technology. Essentially, they estimate a two-stage regression that first examines the impacts of structural variables (trade and technology) on price changes over and above those correlated with industry total factor productivity growth. Next, they retain the coefficients on each structural variable from this first-stage estimation and use them as dependent variables in the change in factor cost shares across industries. This, essentially, aims at isolating the changes in factor prices (wages and rents) that would have occurred if changes in the structural variables (trade and technology) had been the only influence.

This approach is close in spirit to the "mandated" regressions undertaken by Leamer and Krueger, but more carefully parses out the exogenous influence of trade and/or technology on factor prices. Using this specification, Feenstra and Hanson find in their benchmark specifications that trade can account for 15-40% of the rise in the wages of nonproduction (i.e., skilled) workers between 1979 and 1990.

Appendix 1C: Summary of research methodology and findings, and heterodox models

The list below summarizes 30 studies in the trade and wages literature and gives a rough description of their research methodology and findings. The studies are generally grouped together by the methodology with which they were undertaken.

Borjas, Freeman, and Katz (1992, 1997)
Factor content calculations that capture (exclusively) the between-industry impact of trade (and immigration) flows. Trade and immigration combined account for 33-66% of the decline in the wage of dropouts relative to high school (HS) graduates between 1980 and 1995, and 7-14% of the decline in the wages of HS graduates relative to college graduates. Trade alone explains half of the latter effect, but only about 15-20% of the former, accounting for 6-11% of the decline in relative dropout wages. These findings are not "adjusted" for trade deficit impacts, so most of this effect stems from differences between traded and non-traded industries.

Katz and Murphy (1992)
Examination of the vector-product of relative wages and relative labor supplies of 64 separate demographic groupings: sex (2) by experience (8) by education (4). Using CPS microdata, they find that the vector-products are positive—meaning that the same categories that saw relative wage increases also saw relative labor supply growth—implying that a shift in labor demand is the culprit for rising wage inequality. They find substantial contributions made by between-industry labor demand shifts, and find that trade increased the implicit labor supply of dropouts by between 0.63 and 2.2% and reduced the implicit labor supply of college graduates by 0.55 to 1.5% from 1979 to 1985. Given their preferred relative wage elasticity (1.4), this explains roughly 10-15% of the dropout/graduate gap between 1979 and 1985.

Murphy and Welch (1991)
Industry share-shift employment exercise: as the trade deficit widens in the early 1980s, less-skilled workers are displaced in disproporationate numbers from tradeable sectors. They find that the estimated demand impacts from trade-deficit-induced displacement exactly matches the pattern of wage changes by educational group. They do not, however, back out a number on the contribution of trade to overall inequality and only note that the directional impact is consistent with trade making a contribution to inequality.

Wood (1994, 1995)
Begins with basic factor-content calculations, then argues that generic factor contents understate the labor market impacts of trade by not accounting for greater labor intensity in production in developing countries, and by not accounting for the defensive innovation in labor-saving technology spurred by international competi-

tion. Adjusting for these, Wood finds that trade reduces the demand for less-skilled labor by 22% between 1979 and 1989. This translates into trade accounting for 50% of the decline in less-skilled wages over this time period.

Cooper (1994)

Tracks the differential performance of aggregate manufacturing vis-à-vis the apparel, textile, and footwear industries. The latter saw much more rapid employment loss between 1980 and 1990. Comparing this actual loss with a counterfactual that sees these industries losing (less-skilled) jobs only at the same rate as overall manufacturing, Cooper estimates that the relative wage of less-skilled workers would have declined only 90% as far as it actually did between 1980 and 1990, implying a contribution of trade to wage inequality of 10%—even when looking only at apparel, textiles, and footwear, which only employ 15% of less-skilled labor in overall manufacturing. It's tough to know how exactly to scale this up to the entire manufacturing sector as the sectors under examination are a small share of manufacturing employment, but probably a larger share of jobs displaced by trade. But it seems safe to say that the overall impact is at least double that which is found for the apparel, textile, and footwear sectors; this implies trade accounts for roughly 10-20% of the rise in inequality over the 1980s.

Lawrence and Slaughter (1993)

Regression-based analysis of industry prices on industry shares of less-skilled labor; trade theory argues inequality-generating impacts of trade will work through the falling prices of goods that more intensively use less-skilled labor. They find that prices move in the wrong direction over the 1979-89 period.

Sachs and Shatz (1994)

Rebuttal to Lawrence and Slaughter (1993). Argue that the former should have excluded the (very volatile) computer industry from their regressions. This industry has a high share of skilled workers and has seen enormous price declines. With this exclusion, the pattern of price changes fits predictions of Stolper-Samuelson theorem. They find that trade flows between 1978 and 1990 reduced the demand for production workers in manufacturing by 7.2% and increased the demand for nonproduction workers by 2.1%. This 9.3% swing in the relative demand for production workers in manufacturing implies a 1.4% swing in this ratio economy-wide, which translates into a 2% change in this relative wage over that period. Sachs and Shatz (1994) argue that their calculations imply that trade contributed roughly 4-10% to the observed inequality over this time period.

Baldwin and Cain (1997)

Regression-based price estimates. They find associations with rising product prices and rising shares of skilled labor across 79 manufacturing industries. From this, and other results using a factor-content approach, they show that trade can explain between 9% and 13% of the rise in relative skilled wages (which they define as those with any college attendance) from 1977 to 1987.

Leamer (1992, 1996, 1998)
Regression-based price estimates. Finds robust evidence that globalization has been a prime contributor to falling prices for goods whose production is intensive in less-skilled labor. Relatively imprecise point estimates imply a large increase in the wages of professional and technical workers and capital earnings, and a large decrease in the wages of production workers. All told, these results suggest that foreign competition can explain 10-40% of the rise in most metrics of wage inequality (say, production/nonproduction relative wage).

Krueger (1997)
Regression-based price estimates, using better price data than previous studies. Finds that there is strong evidence of falling relative prices in sectors that employ larger shares of less-skilled labor, which is consistent with Stolper-Samuelson effects exacerbating wage inequality. Results suffer, if anything, from showing consistently that trade can account for 100%+ of all the increase in wage inequality between 1989 and 1995.

Mishel and Schmitt (1996)
Regression-based price estimates, using a broad range of skill categories. Find strong evidence for Stolper-Samuelson effects, especially when using education-based skill measures. Depending on the skill-measure used, they find that price effects account for 6-108% of the rise in the relative wages of skilled workers between 1979 and 1989. Their preferred specifications show trade accounting for 8-28% of the (regression-controlled) increase in the college premium.

Feenstra and Hanson (1995, 1999)
The 1995 paper is a rebuttal to Berman, Bound, and Griliches BG (1994), offering a model where trade flows can lead to rising intra-industry shares of skilled labor and confirming the model's predictions with regressions on U.S. manufacturing. Find that rising import shares are strongly correlated with rising shares of skilled labor in industry payrolls. Find that one-third of the rise in manufacturing's skilled labor share is explained by rising import shares. The 1999 paper extends other work on relative price changes and globalization by arguing that only shifts in total factor productivity (tfp) can contain information on decomposing the relative impacts of trade versus technology. Find large but relatively imprecise estimates regarding outsourcing's contribution to wage inequality (often finding that outsourcing over-explains the rise in inequality). The results are fragile, however.

Feenstra, Hanson, and Swenson (2000)
Examine data derived from the 9802 offshore assembly program (OAP) to examine the skill content of production done abroad and imported into the United States. The OAP program allows firms to pay tariffs only on the value-added of goods incurred abroad. It tracks the value-added of goods when they leave the United States and then when they are re-imported. Feenstra et al. (2000) find that off-shored production activities are indeed extensive in the use of unskilled labor, suggesting that patterns of trade in the United States should, in line with classical trade theory, lead to a reduction in the relative demand for less-skilled workers in the United States.

Krugman (1995)
Baseline computable general equilibrium (CGE) model roughly consistent with trade shares in the United States is used to see how much wages would have to change to spur this observed amount of trade, starting from autarky. Finds that 1995 levels of less-developed country (LDC) trade can account for roughly 10% of the total rise in wage inequality since 1980.

Cline (1997)
Extension of the Krugman (1995) CGE model, including many more sectors, countries, and three factors. Finds that expanded trade with LDCs can explain 40% of the rise in the observed wage inequality in the United States between 1980 and 1995.

Harrigan (2000)
Reports the results of using a small-scale general equilibrium model of wages between 1967 and 1995. Harrigan uses relatively short time-series observations on output, wages, capital stocks, and trade flows to fit a reduced-form model of trade and wages. Argues that most of the impact on wage inequality is "domestic" not "international," yet his finding that final product price changes have played a large role in driving wage trends is exactly in the spirit of Stolper-Samuelson trade-induced wage changes, a point that he concedes. Combining Feenstra and Hanson (1999) estimates on what degree of price changes have been caused by international influences with Harrigan's numbers yields the estimate that trade can explain roughly 15% of the rise in inequality from 1980 to 1995.

Bernard and Jensen (1997, 2000)
Plant-level examination of exporting and non-exporting plants. Find that between-plant shifts between exporting and non-exporting plants are the key driver in pay-roll share increases of skilled workers in U.S. manufacturing between 1980 and 1987. Second study focuses on changing patterns of wage inequality within U.S. states. Changing industrial composition, particularly the loss of durable manufacturing jobs, is strongly associated with rising wage inequality.

Berman, Bound, and Griliches (1994)
Regression analysis on the share of skilled labor in manufacturing industry payrolls from 1979 to 1987. Find that much of the rise in skilled labor intensity in manufacturing occurred at the intra-industry level. They take this finding as evidence that trade has not been a primary driver in the rise in relative demand for skilled labor.

Borjas and Ramey (1993, 1995)
Cointegration test of rising trade deficit in manufactured goods and rising wage inequality. Use variation across U.S. metropolitan statistical areas in industrial structure and trade exposure to test the hypothesis that trade flows have both led to a decline in demand for less-skilled workers and deprived them of labor rents in manufacturing. Find that the trade deficit can explain 10-35% of wage inequality between 1979 and 1989.

Mincer (1991)
Wage equations augmented with the trade/GNP ratio and service/manufacturing employment shares. Finds both to be significant in some specifications, but does not decompose the impact of these on total wage inequality and stresses the role of technical change.

Lovely and Richardson (2000)
Regression-based estimates of how industry wage premiums are affected by trade, and particularly by the characteristics of U.S. trade partners. Find estimates that pure industry wage premiums accruing to non-college workers are negatively impacted by large trade flows coming from developing nations. Wage premiums for college-educated workers actually rise, making the industry premium effect exacerbate the more standard distributional consequences of trade.

Heterodox models

Besides those using FCA, PPR, and CGE models, there is a hodgepodge of studies using more heterodox methodological techniques to get a sense of the trade and inequality link. These studies tend to stray a bit away from strict tests of the SST and other mainstream trade theories. Many of these are, however, quite useful in broadening the channels through which trade can impact inequality. Some of these are described below.

One of the most useful heterodox treatments is actually an extension of the HOT model—Robinson and Thierfelder (1996) remedy a key problem in many of the "pure" trade models by introducing room for a non-traded good. In many trade models, every good is assumed to be either an export- or an import-competing good. In the U.S. economy, one imagines that at least half of domestic production is not tradeable (think restaurants, salons, health care workers, etc.). Given the bulk of the non-traded sector, it seems like the effects of trade on domestic labor markets will be attenuated. Robinson and Thierfelder (1996) introduce non-traded goods in an ingenious way and provide some useful ways to decompose the effects of trade on wages. One of the more realistic empirical portions of their model is the ratcheting down of the "magnification effect" relative to models where all goods are traded: it still exists, but it tends to not multiply the impacts of trade by orders of magnitude the way traditional magnification effects can. Their "1223" model is used in Chapter 3 (and explained there in some detail) to update earlier estimates in the trade and wages debate.

One of the most famous non-HOT arguments in the trade and wages debate relates to a claim by Rodrik (1998), who argues that trade *flattens* the demand curve for labor in all countries. This flattening occurs because liberalization allows firms to substitute foreign producers and labor for domestic labor more easily, meaning that demand for domestic labor is more *elastic*—any given *wage* increase for labor will lead to larger employment losses for this group than before global integration

This has large implications. For one, policy interventions aimed at helping the working class population in the global North are often financed through payroll taxes (Social Security and part of Medicare are financed by payroll taxes in the United States, for example). One consequence of more elastic labor demand is that the burden of this labor market taxation (income and payroll taxes) falls more heavily on workers and less heavily on firms, making tax policy less redistributive after liberalization. While the working class may still receive benefit from government spending, they also bear a larger burden of taxation that supports this spending.

Slaughter (2001) empirically assesses Rodrik's argument by examining the manufacturing sector of the United States for evidence that industries experiencing the largest increase in trade flows are also those demonstrating a rising elasticity of labor demand. He finds suggestive evidence that the elasticity of demand for production labor has increased in line with foreign competition, but little evidence that the same holds true for nonproduction and supervisory labor. His results, however, are statistically very fragile, and the inclusion of a time trend makes international trade insignificant as a determinant of labor demand elasticity. That is, while it is clearly true that the demand for some grades of labor has become more elastic over time, it is not clear that this increase is being driven by international trade. That said, this is, again, a suggestive result.

Senses (2006) extends Slaughter's (2001) initial work by using plant-level data from the Census Bureau. She finds "heavy outsourcing" industries saw significant increases in the labor demand elasticity for production workers during the 1980s. The Senses finding is quite robust to changes in regression specification, and the precise measure of international competitive pressures used. Senses also finds that as the share of production labor in total industry value-added shrank over time (and this happened dramatically in U.S. manufacturing over the past two decades), the rise in the elasticity of labor demand began to reverse in the early 1990s, although it does not retreat back to its early 1980s levels.

The evidence on labor demand elasticity suggests that globalization may not just pressure the share of income accruing to labor; it also flattens the labor demand curve, making redistributive policy interventions aimed at helping this group less tenable, and reducing their bargaining power by making compensation increases more costly in employment terms. In short, at the same time that globalization increases the demand for social insurance interventions and policy interventions to increase workers' bargaining power (increasing inequality), it can also make these harder to supply (by making policy interventions and aggressive wage bargaining more costly).

The elasticities studies referenced above are one example of how trade restricts the range of possibilities for the bargains workers can strike with employers. Essentially, if labor demand elasticity rises, any given wage increase will carry much larger employment costs than before. A couple of other studies have tried to get at even more direct measures of the impact of trade on labor's bargaining power as well.

Choi (2003) looks at the union wage premium in industries in the U.S. manufacturing sector. He interprets large stocks of foreign direct investment (FDI) in industries as adding to the "credibility" of threats to relocate production abroad and further argues that this enhanced credibility on the part of firms' threats will lead to a lower union wage premium. Using industry-level panel data that cover 1983-96, Choi finds a significant effect of outward FDI on industry union wage premiums: the elasticity of union wage premium with respect to FDI is -0.33 to -0.5. This reduction in the union wage premium has large wage effects for workers in the industries that have large stocks of FDI. Choi finds that unionized workers in the highest FDI industry (soaps and cleaners) have wages that are 18% less than nonunionized workers in industries with no FDI, even after accounting for individual demographic and educational characteristics.

In my own work (Bivens 2006), I examine the ability of workers in U.S. manufacturing industries to claim some share of industry surplus. Essentially, I examine the correlation between an industry's profits per worker and wages, controlling for worker characteristics. I find that, from 1967 to 1983, there was a strong and significant correlation between these two measures, with higher industry profits correlated with higher wages in succeeding years. Post-1983, this correlation becomes insignificant. However, when I make an adjustment to measures of industry profitability in this latter period to account for the improved fallback position of firms in different industries based on the ease of substituting foreign labor and goods for domestic workers, this correlation returns. Essentially, a much smaller share of an industry's profits are up for grabs between employers and workers in the latter period, and this shrinking share is directly related to the ease with which firms can substitute away from domestic workers. This breakdown in the ability of labor to claim some measure of industry surplus has non-trivial impacts, resulting in manufacturing wages by 1996 that are over 2% lower than they would have been absent this decline in bargaining power.

Tang and Wood (1997) provide another extension to the HOT portfolio of theories that seems particularly relevant to today's global economy. They argue that falling trade and "cooperation costs" between nations have eroded the implicit monopoly Northern labor had in working with Northern capital. That is, a portion of wages for workers in the United States reflects the fact that they were able to work with a world-class capital stock (both machines and human capital) that wasn't available to the rest of the world. As barriers to trade (both political and technological) fall, this monopoly power is eroded: American autoworkers, for example, know that GM can place plants in Canada, Mexico, or China, and they no longer can enjoy a monopoly of GM's capital stock. To keep GM from moving, they must accept a lower wage than would otherwise prevail. Owners of capital, conversely, earn higher returns as a result of falling trade and cooperation costs: they now have a much larger pool of "bidders" to choose from.

Dinopolous and Segerstrom (1999) put forward a model that shows global (not just domestic) trade liberalization increasing the return to research and development activities by allowing firms that invest in R&D to earn resulting monopoly profits over a larger global market. If R&D activities are capital-intensive (which seems natural), then liberalization increases the return to capital and reduces the return to labor. Dinopolous and Segrestrom argue that time series evidence argues strongly that trade liberalization and resulting increases in trade flows look to be the dominant explanation for rising wage inequality in the United States.

Goldberg and Tracy (2001) is the culmination of a long research project examining the way U.S. labor markets adjust to changes in the dollar exchange rate. Given the enormous volatility in this exchange rate, it would be surprising if it did not induce wrenching labor market adjustments. The surprising finding of Goldberg and Tracy is that it is wages, not employment, that seem to bear the largest brunt of exchange rate adjustment. Dollar appreciations cause costly job loss to less-skilled workers and depress wages for even those workers who do not experience job loss. Skilled workers who do not change jobs during dollar appreciation see significant wage gains. Further, the impact of dollar depreciations and appreciations are not symmetric; for skilled workers wage growth accelerates during times of dollar appreciations but does not then fall during times of dollar depreciations. In a striking finding, Goldberg and Tracy estimate that more than half of the change in one measure of wage inequality (the ratio of high school graduates to dropout wages) can be accounted for by exchange rate changes that occurred in this time.

As startling as these results are, they gain even more strength when combined with the findings of Ruhl (2003). Ruhl argues that the influence of "permanent" changes—either commitments to trade liberalization through international agreements or falling costs induced by technology change—have much larger impacts on trade flows than "transitory" ones, like exchange rate movements. If this is the case, the Goldberg and Tracy (2001) effects noted above will be amplified when applied to permanent changes like trade policy reducing market access barriers. Falling tariffs (or other trade costs) are akin to dollar appreciations (both make imports less expensive for domestic consumers), so the asymmetric effects of dollar appreciations tracked by Goldberg and Tracy (2001) (job loss and wage suppression for less-skilled workers and wage growth for skilled workers) would, logically, be even stronger in response to these long-run, structural policy changes.

The last, and probably most provocative, of the extensions to standard trade theory comes from Davis (1998). A number of writers have looked at rising wage inequality in the United States and unemployment rates in western European economies throughout the 1980s as different institutional responses to a common economic shock. Whether the shock is an increase in trade flows from LDCs or global changes in technology that favor skilled workers and capital, the argument runs that wage flexibility in the United States has kept this shock from causing unemployment, but at the expense of rising inequality. Conversely, in Western Europe, binding minimum wages (and other compensation supports) kept the shock from leading to inequality, but only at the expense of rising unemployment. Davis, however, puts forward a model that posits the United States and Europe as integrated economies whose responses jointly determine outcomes after an economic shock. As long as one economy (Europe's) is committed to binding minimum wages, the more flexible economy (the United States) is *entirely insulated* from the shock of rising trade flows from LDCs. Davis argues that Europe's ability to withstand high unemployment props up American wages and provides a buffer against the full extent of globalization's pressures.

Appendix 1D: Recent advances in FCA (or Wood was (mostly) right)

The Wood (1994) insight was controversial enough that almost no subsequent research used his technique in the first round of the trade and wages debate. Borjas, Freeman, and Katz (1997) accept Wood's general insight in their own work, but make a much more modest adjustment to their own measurement, essentially using the input-output technology that existed roughly a decade previous in the United States to measure the contemporary labor content of imports. Using this adjustment, they find that trade accounts for a bit under 10% of the rise in the ratio of wages for workers with a four-year college degree relative to the wages of those with a high school diploma only. Borjas, Freeman, and Katz (1997) made clear that the degree to which one follows the strict Wood (1994) adjustment will greatly impact one's assessment of the true factor content of U.S. trade.

As noted in Chapter 3, recent empirical literature focusing on the factor content of trade more generally (not related to the trade and wages debate) has largely vindicated Wood's insight. This new line of research has its roots in perhaps the oldest finding in empirical trade economics—the "Leontief Paradox." In 1953, future Nobelist Wasily Leontief, using data on *American* production techniques (input-output tables), concluded that, contrary to expectations rooted in the factor proportions approach to trade, American imports were not labor intensive, and American exports were not capital intensive. Subsequent work generally confirmed the Leontief Paradox, and noted that the implication of this work was that net trade flows had little impact on relative factor supplies, hence little impact on relative wages or inequality. Trefler (1995) even termed this result "the case of the missing trade," as the measured factor content of U.S. trade seems to show essentially *zero* net exchange of factor services through imports and exports.

The key theoretical insight that led to an eventual overturning of the Leontief Paradox came through jettisoning the assumption (crucial to the FPET) that every country had access to identical production techniques and common technology. Once it was allowed that different nations were working off different production possibility frontiers, the inevitable result was that empirical measurement could not rely on a single country's (the United States') input-output technology for measuring the factor content of trade.

In a later paper, Trefler (2003) demonstrates this point theoretically by demonstrating that international differences in production techniques lead inevitably to the clear prediction that the relevant factor content of trade is based on the number of factors *worldwide* that are used to produce a country's trade flows, a point made previously by Deardorff (1982) that never was properly integrated into the trade and wages debate.

Davis and Weinstein (2003a, 2003b), in a series of papers that make use of internationally comparable input-output tables, have been most responsible for moving the ball forward on the measurement front. They find that extending the

HOT to allow for different production techniques and technology between countries yields estimates that the factor content of American trade is much larger than when using only U.S. production techniques in estimation and that the pattern of these factor contents is firmly in line with the predictions of the HOT: U.S. imports are clearly labor intensive while exports are just as clearly skills/capital intensive.

Feenstra and Hanson (2000) empirically test another possibility raised by Davis and Weinstein (2001): even measuring the factor content of U.S. exports with U.S. input-output tables can result in estimates biased downward. The intuition is that even narrowly defined "export" industries in the United States are composed of a number of quite heterogenous firms. The firms most likely to export almost surely use more skills- and capital-intensive production techniques than other firms in the same industry that produce only for the home market. Using industry-average input-output relationships to predict the skill and capital intensity of U.S. exports, in short, leads to an understatement of the factor content of trade. Feenstra and Hanson (2000) find that this aggregation bias is large.

Appendix 1E: Leamer vs. Krugman and PPR

The appropriateness of PPR as an estimating technique has been most comprehensively debated by Krugman (2000) and Leamer (2000). My own view on the question of PPR absolutism mirrors Krugman (2000). In short, Leamer (2000) is right in asserting that strict readings of the SST show that it only links trade prices (not volumes) and factor prices directly. He is also right in arguing that exogenous changes in global prices will filter into changes in domestic factor prices. Where he's wrong is that PPR is the *only way* (or even the most reliable way) to answer the larger question (usefully phrased by Deardorff and Hakura (1994)) of "what would American wages be *but for* the ability to import labor-intensive goods from LDCs?"

On this question, Krugman (2000) offers the best summation:

> In other words, the economist trying to analyze the effects of trade on wages is not faced with the textbook problem of predicting the effect of a given change in goods prices on factor prices. Instead, the problem is how to infer the impact of trade, as opposed to other influences, on goods prices—only then can one calculate the implied factor price effect. And once one realizes that the issue is one of inference rather than a question about the mechanics of the model, one also realizes that the volume of trade is not irrelevant or immaterial; it is a crucial piece of evidence. (Krugman 2000)

Theoretical issues aside, the results of PPR regressions are not encouraging for those looking for real precision about the impact of trade on American wages.

Krueger (1997) finds generally supportive evidence linking trade and wage inequality through PPR, and most of his specifications find that the implicit trade effects *overexplain* the rise in inequality in the 1990s.

Mishel and Schmitt (1996) undertake an exhaustive check of the robustness of the link between price declines and less-skilled labor intensity, and find that in the majority of specifications trade explains a very significant part (from 6% to over 70%) of the rise in wage inequality over the 1980s and early 1990s (the wideness of their estimates reflects their use of several different skill-cuts). Sachs and Shatz (1994) and Baldwin and Cain (1994, 1997) find significant impacts of PPR and estimate that it contributes 4-15% of the total rise in wage inequality over the period being studied.

Conversely, a much smaller number of PPR studies have failed to show any impact of globalization on inequality. Lawrence and Slaughter (1993) is notable in arguing, based on PPR specifications, that there exists *no* evidence of a significant relationship between trade and rising wage inequality. These results, however, are very closely linked to the Sachs and Shatz (1994) results showing non-trivial trade effects. The main difference between the studies is the treatment of a single industry—the production of computing equipment. This industry is quite capital intensive and saw extraordinarily rapid price declines over recent decades. Much of these price declines, however, are the result of an imputation made by the Bureau of Labor Statistics to account for the rising quality of computing equipment over time. Adjusting for quality in price indices is clearly the correct thing to do, but the magnitude of the quality adjustment has been questioned by many.

Slaughter (1998), besides presenting an excellent overview of the methodological issues raised by PPR studies, undertakes a quick bit of original analysis to re-examine the Krueger (1997) results for the early 1990s. He finds mixed results, but in his preferred specification with all manufacturing industries (Krueger 1997 just used a sub-set of manufacturing) he finds little evidence for product price effects on wages. However, of the four studies identified by Slaughter (1998) as being exemplary for linking theory most closely to empirics (Leamer 1996; Baldwin and Cain 1997; Krueger 1997; and Feenstra and Hanson 1999) all find significant and large effects of product price changes on wages, with the average of their intervals implying that these product price changes accounted for roughly 15-45% of the total rise in wage inequality during the periods studied.

The most recent and the most careful of the PPR studies is Feenstra and Hanson (1999). They use PPR to decompose the impacts of trade and technology on relative wages. They explicitly try to measure the separate effects of trade and technology on changes in industry prices, which has been a key weakness of this literature (outside of Leamer's efforts, anyway). Their preferred specifications suggest that trade (which they measure as international "outsourcing," or the share of intermediate inputs that are imported) can account for 15-40% of the rise in the wages of nonproduction (skilled) workers relative to production (less-skilled) workers.

Appendix 1F: Another CGE model

Harrigan (2000) has estimated a CGE model whose complexity lies somewhere between that of Krugman and Cline's. Harrigan doesn't back out a number for trade's contribution to inequality explicitly, and concludes the paper with an assertion that "most" of the causes of inequality are domestic, not international. Yet, his model results, read carefully, suggest a significant possible role for trade in driving inequality.

Specifically, he finds that a 10% reduction in prices for less-skilled labor-intensive goods should raise the wages of college graduates relative to high school graduates by roughly 3.5%. From 1980 to 1995 the relative price of high-skill intensive goods rose by over 30%, suggesting that the relative price effects are responsible for well over a third of the rise in wage inequality during this time.

Harrigan rejects a trade-based explanation for these falling relative prices on two bases. The first is that an import price variable is not statistically significant in a regression of the share of GNP claimed by less-skilled workers. The second is that a portion of the large relative price declines are driven by services, which he argues are not likely to be affected much by international trade.

The first measure seems to be asking a bit too much of a single regression, based on quite aggregated data. In fact, the *domestic* price measures in the same regression are statistically insignificant as well. On the second point, many of the services pointed to by Harrigan in driving large price changes are actually quite tradeable, most notably the finance and insurance sectors.

Harrigan grants that international effects could well contribute to the pattern of falling prices for goods whose production is less-skilled labor-intensive—"until we understand the causes of these price changes, we cannot rule out an important rule for import competition."

Feenstra and Hanson (1999), on the way to doing the PPR analysis referenced above, shed some light on the relationship between patterns of price changes and globalization. They examine the relationship between industry price changes and various measures of international "outsourcing" and investment in high-technology capital as a way to differentiate between domestic (technology) and international (trade) effects on relative prices. They find that outsourcing measures are correlated with price changes, explaining about half as much of a given industry's price change as technology. Combining this rough estimate with Harrigan's (2000) results on price changes and inequality would lead to the conclusion that the Harrigan (2000) study essentially supports an estimate of trade's contribution to wage inequality of around 15%.

Appendix 1G: Cline's results and shares of inequality

Cline (1997) reports results from his TIDE model as trade accounting for 18% of the rise in wage inequality, but a close reading of his book shows that this 18% is actually trade's contribution to the *gross* rise in inequality, an esoteric concept not cited by any other of the reviewed studies on inequality. This gross rise is essentially the rise in inequality *that would have occurred absent any other countervailing influence*. The 1973-93 period (that studied by Cline) saw a very rapid increase in the average educational attainment of the U.S. workforce; this educational upgrading leaned hard against the gross rise in inequality and resulted in a net rise that was much smaller than the gross rise (although obviously still quite large).

The net increase in inequality is essentially the rise that we observe in the final data. Using this number as the baseline (which is the standard for every other study in the trade and wages debate and the inequality literature in general) suggests that trade can account for well over a third of the rise in wage inequality over this time.

Appendix 1H: Full specifications of Krugman and the 1223 models

Krugman

The early 1990s saw a flurry of papers on the topic of trade and wage inequality, driven largely by the debate over NAFTA. Krugman (1995) offered his simple CGE model as an illustrative exercise to obtain an estimate of the correct order of magnitude about trade's impact on inequality within wage incomes.

His results suggested that trade flows could explain about 10% of the entire rise in wage inequality that had characterized the previous decades. The relative modesty of this effect was a direct result of the facts that (1) trade flows still remained a relatively small part of the U.S. economy, and (2) trade flows with LDCs, the type that seemed most relevant to generating inequality, remained a relatively small part of total U.S. trade flows.

The twist of the current model is that instead of using actual trade data, it instead uses a variety of forecasts about the extent and reach of offshoring over the next decade to provide a rough estimate as to how much this will affect U.S. incomes. The final results sketch out the changes in relative returns to labor and the returns to skills, capital, and credentials consistent with the various forecasts of offshoring's reach in the U.S. economy.

The model itself is a simple excel spreadsheet available from the author upon request. The essential elements are as follows.

The model is a 2x2x2 model (two countries, two goods, and two factors of production), with skills and labor being the factors of production. Good 1 is skills intensive and is produced and exported by the United States to the rest of the world (ROW). Good 2 is labor intensive and is imported from the ROW to the United States.

The following assumptions are used in the model:

Initial ratio of earnings of labor and skills: 1 to 2
Share of skills in industry 1 employment: 0.5
Share of skills in industry 2 employment: 0.2
Share of skills-earnings in national income: 0.4

Given these, the following parameters fall out as residuals:

Share of skills payments in industry 1 value-added: 2/3
Share of skills payments in industry 2 value-added: 1/3
Share of good 1 in total expenditure: 5/7

All prices (including factor prices) are normalized to 1, with the earnings of labor being the numeraire. To make this work, asset units are measured as halves, so that the initial endowment is set at 70 units of labor and 60 (halves of) skills.

The production for each good is modeled as a standard constant elasticity of substitution (CES) function of the form:

(1) $X_i = [\delta_{hi} H_i^{-\rho} + \delta_{li} L_i^{-\rho}]^{-1/\rho}$

Here X is the output of good i, while δ is the "distribution parameter" associated with factors of production H (skills) and L (labor) respectively. The parameter measures the substitutability of skills and labor in production and is related to the elasticity of substitution by the relation, where is the elasticity of substitution.

Given (1), the unit cost function can then be derived:

(2) $c(w_h, w_l) = [\delta_{xh}^{1/1+\rho} w_h^{\rho/(1+\rho)} + \delta_{li}^{1/(1+\rho)} w_l^{\rho/(1+\rho)}]^{1+1/\rho}$

Here, w represents the return to skills (h) and labor (l), respectively.
Lastly, the factor demand for unit output can be obtained (for skills):

(3) $a_{hi} = ((1 + \rho / \rho))[\delta_{si}^{1/(1+\rho)} [\delta_{si}^{1/(1+\rho)} w_h^{\rho/(1+\rho)} + \delta_{li}^{1/(1+\rho)} w_l^{\rho/(1+\rho)}]^{1/\rho} w^{1+\rho}$

From here, output of both goods can be determined by the requirement that both skills and labor are fully employed, hence:

(4) $H = a_{h1} X_1 + a_{h2} X_2$

$L = a_{l1} X_1 + a_{l2} X_2$

which yields:

(5) $X_1 = D^{-1}[a_{l2} H - a_{h2} L], X_2 = D^{-1}[-a_{l1} H + a_{h1} L]$

where $D = a_{h1} a_{l2} - a_{h2} a_{l1}$

Given the output and prices (unit costs) of each good, the trade vector is just the share of trade in U.S. output, or the difference between the share of good 1 in output and in consumption:

(6) $T = P_1 X_1 / (P_1 X_1 + P_2 X_2) - 4/7$

In the initial setup, with all prices normalized at 1, the T vector is 0—all of the output of both industries is consumed.

The strategy for the estimates in this paper, following directly from Krugman (1995), is to then change the relative return of skills (raising it). This increases the output of good 1 (the asset-intensive good) and decreases the output of good 2 (the labor-intensive good). The Cobb-Douglas consumption function, however, insures that the share of total expenditure (consumption) on each good remains the same. Hence, some of good 1 is exported and some of good 2 is imported. The upshot is that for every level of trade shares in GDP, there is a corresponding (and unique) change in relative earnings associated with it. It is these results that are reported in the paper.

1223 model

The 1223 model assumes that the economy produces two goods, E (exports) and D (domestically consumed). The economy also consumes two goods, D (above) and M (imports). M and D are imperfect substitutes for U.S. consumers. Aggregate spending in the U.S. economy is a function of imports (M), domestic production (D), and the ease of substitution between these goods (known as the Armington elasticity of substitution).

U.S. consumers' desired ratio of imports to domestic goods depends on the price of each (P^m, P^D) and this Armington elasticity of substitution between them.

$$(1) \quad \frac{M}{D} = \left(\frac{P^d}{P^m} \right)^{\sigma_q}$$

Robinson and Thiererfelder (1996) follow Jones (1965) in specifying the technology for producing E and D by the following coefficients matrix A:

$$(2) \quad A = \begin{vmatrix} A_{se} & A_{sd} \\ A_{le} & A_{ld} \end{vmatrix}$$

In each case, A_i is the quantity of a given factor (labor or education) needed to produce a unit of good j. Given this matrix, and an assumption of full-employment (all labor and all education in the economy are profitably employed), we get the following expressions:

$$(3) \quad A_{se}E + A_{sd}D = S$$
$$A_{le}E + A_{ld}D = L$$

Assuming competitive markets, unit costs in D and E production will equal market prices, and will be exhausted by payments to factors of production (S and L), yielding the following two equations:

(4) $A_{se}W_s + A_{le}W_l = P^e$

$\qquad A_{sd}W_s + A_{ld}W_l = P^d$

Finally, to close the model, Robinson and Thiererfelder have the following equation for the trade balance.

(5) $P^m M = \Phi P^e E$

Here, Φ is a parameter giving the ratio of import expenditures to export earnings. When this value is one, exports and imports balance, and the usual HOT conclusions apply. An increase in Φ implies a deteriorating trade balance.

Assuming that tradeable prices are set on global markets, so far we have seven independent equations for seven endogenous variables: Q, E, D, M, W_s, W_p, and P^d.

Beyond these endogenous variables, another set of structural parameters need to be specified to trace out the impact of trade (changing world prices, more specifically) on relative wages.

First, define as the share of the total supply of factor i used in sector j:

(6) $\lambda_{se} = {}^{A_{se}E}\!/_S ; \lambda_{sd} = {}^{A_{sd}}\!/_S$

$\qquad \lambda_{le} = {}^{A_{le}E}\!/_L ; \lambda_{ld} = {}^{A_{ld}}\!/_L$

Next, define θ_{ij} as the share of factor i in total income generated in sector j:

(7) $\theta_{ij} = \dfrac{A_{ij}W_{ij}}{P^j}$

Given that factors are fully employed and all income must accrue to one or the other factor this gives us:

(8) $\displaystyle\sum_j \lambda_{ij} = \sum_i \theta_{ij} = 1$

We can define the following matrices:

$$(9) \quad \gamma = \begin{vmatrix} \lambda_{se} & \lambda_{sd} \\ \lambda_{le} & \lambda_{ld} \end{vmatrix}; \qquad \theta = \begin{vmatrix} \theta_{se} & \theta_{sd} \\ \theta_{le} & \theta_{ld} \end{vmatrix}$$

Given that the rows of each of these must sum to one, their determinants are given by:

$$(10) \quad |\lambda| = \lambda_{se} - \lambda_{le};$$

$$(11) \quad |\theta| = \theta_{se} - \theta_{le}$$

Since E is assumed to be more skills intensive than D, this implies that both determinants are positive and less than one.

Using lower-case to denote the relative change in a variable or parameter, the elasticities of substitution between skills and labor in production in the two sectors E and D can be defined by:

$$(12) \quad \sigma_e = \frac{a_{le} - a_{se}}{w_s - w_l}; \qquad\qquad \sigma_d = \frac{a_{ld} - a_{sd}}{w_s - w_l}$$

Robinson and Thiererfelder define two additional parameters, which Jones defines as the "aggregate percentage saving in labor inputs at unchanged outputs associated with a 1% rise in the relative wage rate, the saving resulting from the adjustment to less labor-intensive techniques in both industries as the relative wage rises"

$$(13) \quad \delta_s = \lambda_{se}\theta_{se}\sigma_e + \lambda_{sd}\theta_{sd}\sigma_d$$

$$(14) \quad \delta_l = \lambda_{le}\theta_{le}\sigma_e + \lambda_{ld}\theta_{ld}\sigma_d$$

Finally, the elasticity of transformation (Ω) between E and D is given by:

$$(15) \quad \Omega = \frac{(\delta_s - \delta_l)}{|\lambda| * |\theta|}$$

From this point, the model reduces to four relationships between price changes, production, demand, and relative wage changes. The first is the relationship between relative prices and relative wages along the production possibility frontier:

(16) $(w_s - w_l) = \dfrac{1}{|\theta|} * (p^e - p^d)$

This is the classic Stolper-Samuelson theorem: relative wage changes are equal to relative price changes divided by a magnifier that is the determinant of $|\theta|$, and because this determinant is always less than one, relative wage changes are greater than relative price changes.

The second relationship is movement along the production possibility frontier determined by relative price changes and changes in the endowments of factors of production (skills and labor).

(17) $(e - d) = \dfrac{1}{|\lambda|} * (s - l) + \Omega(p^e - p^d)$

This equation is the Rybycnski theorem. Changes in factor endowments cause (magnified) changes in production between E and D.

On the demand side, log-differentiating equation (1) yields:

(18) $(m - d) = -\sigma_q(p^m - p^d)$

which shows how demand for M and D trades off with changes in relative prices.

Finally, supply and demand are linked through the balance of trade equation (5). Log-differentiating this yields:

(19) $(e - m) = p^m - p^e - \Phi$

Eliminating d in equations (17) and (18), and substituting for e and m in equation (19) yields an expression for changes in the relative prices of D and E as a function of changes in exogenous world prices, factor endowments, and the balance of trade.

(20) $(p^e - p^d) = \dfrac{1}{(\sigma_q + \Omega)} * \left[(\sigma_q - 1) * (p^e - p^d) - \Phi + \dfrac{1}{|\lambda|} * (l - s) \right]$

In this model, when world prices are fixed, is the relative price of non-traded goods to traded goods, and hence is the real exchange rate.

Finally, substituting equation (16) into equation (20) gives us the following equation relating changes in relative wages to changes in world prices, the balance of trade, and factor endowments.

$$(21)\ (w_s - w_l) = \frac{1}{|\theta| * (\sigma_q + \Omega)} * \left[(\sigma_q - 1) * (p^e - p^m) - \Phi + \frac{1}{|\lambda|} * (l - s) \right]$$

If the elasticity of substitution in consumption (the Armington elasticity) goes to infinity (an implicit assumption of classical HOT theorems), this equation collapses back to the traditional Stolper-Samuelson theorem.

$$(22)\ (w_s - w_l) = \frac{1}{|\theta|}(p^e - p^m)$$

Ignoring endowment changes and the balance of trade for a second gives us the following expression:

$$(23)\ (w_s - w_{\cdot}) = \frac{1}{|\theta|} + \left[\frac{(\sigma_q - 1)}{(\sigma_q + \Omega)} \right] * (p^e - p^m)$$

Since is positive, the second term in this expression is always less than one, which results in a great reduction in the Stolper-Samuelson "magnification effect." This reduction stems from the introduction of the non-traded sector D, which greatly reduces the extreme divergence in production and consumption that is implied in most HOT models.

All in all, the 1223 model ably addresses some concerns about the extreme nature of some assumptions in HOT models. It should be noted that the Krugman (1995) CGE model used in the previous section actually manages to avoid many of these extreme problems by relating relative wage changes to the share of trade in GDP. However, the 1223 model allows some additional influences (the trade balance) over and above those of the Krugman (1995) model to influence relative wages.

Table A1-1 shows the data values and parameters that led to the summary results presented in the main text. The model (in the form of an Excel spreadsheet) is available from the author upon request.

TABLE A1-1. Key data and parameters from the 1223 model

		Levels			Changes		
		1989	2000	2005	1989-2000	2000-05	1989-2005
(1)	Export price index, pe	92.7	100.0	109.6	7.83%	9.61%	18.19%
(2)	Import price index, pm	96.0	100.0	104.2	4.23%	4.17%	8.58%
(3)	Non-BA share of labor force, l	76.6	72.5	70.9	-4.10%	-1.60%	-5.70%
(4)	BA share of labor force, s	23.4	27.5	29.1	4.10%	1.60%	5.70%
(5)	Ratio of imports to exports, tb	1.2	1.3	1.6	17.09%	20.39%	37.48%
(6)	Value of the dollar, $	93.0	104.9	98.3	12.80%	-6.33%	5.66%
(7)	College wage, ws	21.9	22.7	25.4	3.83%	12.05%	16.34%
(8)	Non-college wage, wl	12.8	12.6	13.7	-1.46%	9.25%	7.66%
	Change in relative measures						
(1-2)	pe-pm				3.6%	5.4%	9.6%
(3-4)	l-s				-8.2%	-3.2%	-11.4%
(5)	tb				17.1%	20.4%	37.5%
(6)	dollar				12.8%	-6.3%	5.7%
(7-8)	ws-wl				5.3%	2.8%	8.7%

Assumed parameters

Magnification/absorbtion effects	0.09
Prices	0.61
Trade balance	-0.09
Endowments	1.20

Contribution to relative wage change

	1989-2000	2000-05	1989-2005
Import - export prices	2.2%	3.3%	5.9%
Changing trade balance	-1.6%	-1.9%	-3.5%
Changing labor force composition	-9.8%	-3.8%	-13.6%

Actual change in college/non-college wage

	1989-2000	2000-05	1989-2005
	7.4%	0.9%	8.3%

Share of total change

	1989-2000	2000-05	1989-2005
Import - export prices	29.7%	368.7%	70.7%
Changing trade balance	-21.7%	-212.9%	-42.4%
Total trade impact	8.0%	155.8%	28.2%
Changing labor force composition	-33.0%	-1.0%	-19.3%

Source: Author's calculation as described in Appendix 2.

APPENDIX 2

Translating jobs forecasts to trade shares

To get the share of jobs potentially offshorable in 2000, the share of trade flows (the average of imports and exports) in industry shipments was multiplied by employment in these industries. The trade data and industry shipment data are from the Bureau of Economic Analysis (BEA), while the employment counts are from the Bureau of Labor Statistic (BLS).

The reverse calculation is performed to translate the jobs identified as potentially offshorable into implied trade flows in industry shipments—the parameter needed for the estimates of trade's impacts on labor markets.

It should be noted that any possible bias in this is probably downward. Manufacturing workers produce much more output per worker than service employees. So, a given dollar of trade flows is associated with fewer jobs in manufacturing than in services. Manufacturing flows dominated imports and exports in 2000, so applying the ratio of trade flows and employment from 2000 to the coming decade will probably underestimate the impact of offshoring on U.S. labor markets.

In 2000, trade flows equaled 49% of goods output and 4% of services output. Multiplying this by employment in these sectors yields 15.6 million jobs that are potentially offshorable. Forrester Research reports that 315,000 jobs were actually offshored in services in 2003. This represents about 2% of all potentially offshorable jobs. By 2015, Forrester reports that 1.6 million jobs will (annually) be offshored. Assuming that the ease of offshoring remains the same over that time, this implies 75 million potentially offshorable jobs. Assuming that the ease of offshoring doubles over that time (so that 4% of the potentially offshorable jobs actually leave) implies that about 38 million jobs are potentially offshorable.

Given that Forrester stresses the factors making it easier to offshore jobs over time, we use the latter estimate in this chapter, and this implies that about 20 million *additional* jobs will be offshorable in 2015 as compared to today, an estimate a bit higher than but largely in line with the estimates of the other studies in this group.

APPENDIX 3

Quotes on offshoring as more of the same trade

"Outsourcing is just a new way of doing international trade. More things are tradable than were tradable in the past. And that's a good thing."

— N. Gregory Mankiw,
chairman of President Bush's Council of Economic Advisors
(http://www.whitehouse.gov/cea/economic_report_20040210.html)

"As long as the American workforce retains its high level of skills and remains flexible as firms position themselves to improve their productivity, the high-value portion of the service sector will not evaporate."

— Doug Irwin, Robert E. Maxwell '23 Professor of Arts and Sciences, Dartmouth College ("Outsourcing Is Good for America," *Wall Street Journal,* January 28, 2004)

"As with putting together hardware, building software systems is likely to happen locally. There will be less demand for basic programming and more demand for higher-value, higher-paid systems integration."

— Virginia Postrel ("A Researcher Sees an Upside in the Outsourcing of Programming Jobs," *New York Times,* "Economic Scene," January 29, 2004

"There is also no evidence that jobs in the high-value-added sector are migrating overseas. One thing that has made offshore outsourcing possible is the standardization of such business tasks as data entry, accounting, and IT support. The parts of production that are more complex, interactive, or innovative—including, but not limited to, marketing, research, and development—are much more difficult to shift abroad."

— Daniel Drezner, professor of political science, Tufts University ("The Outsourcing Bogeyman," *Foreign Affairs*, May/June 2004)

"Moreover, these highest-earning occupations appear to be in the same sectors where U.S. international trade comparative advantage is observed."

— Catherine Mann, senior fellow, Peterson Institute for International Economics (*Accelerating the Globalization of America*, Peterson Institute for International Economics)

"Even though some IT tasks will be done abroad, many more jobs will be created in America, and higher-paying ones to boot."

— *Economist* editorial, February 23, 2004

"In particular, imagine a country which is relatively abundant in skilled labor, like the United States, and begins to trade with a country which is relatively abundant in unskilled labor, like India. In such a case, trade may increase the real income of skilled labor in the United States and lower that of unskilled labor....Nothing changes in such an analysis of commercial policy when we consider outsourcing."

— Jagdish Bhagwati, Arvind Panagariya, and T.N. Srinivasan ("The Muddles Over Outsourcing," *Journal of Economic Perspectives,* Volume 18(4), 2004)

APPENDIX 4

The gains from trade liberalization: how big and who gets them?

The bulk of this book addresses the effects of global integration, without much discussion about *why* this integration occurred. For decades, a bipartisan consensus that barriers to global integration should be torn down has dominated American politics. While not the only reason, or perhaps even the dominant one, for the rapid surge in trade flows between the United States and its poorer trading partners, it is undeniable that policy (epitomized by agreements like NAFTA and the WTO) aided this integration.

Now that this integration has become politically contested, proponents of the globalization status quo have mounted a defense of this policy consensus. This defense often includes estimates of how much the U.S. economy has gained (or will gain) by cutting barriers to trade (or *trade liberalization* in the policy jargon).

Too many of these estimates are clearly inflated beyond any number that would (or at least should) be blessed by mainstream economics, yet they have been deeply influential to the public debate. This appendix will take a long look at an example of two numbers that have been hugely important in the contemporary trade debate: $1 trillion and $500 billion.

The first number ($1 trillion) is a purported measure of how much *past* trade agreements have added to the U.S. economy. Sometimes this $1 trillion is divided by the number of American households to argue that trade has added $9,000-10,000 to the typical household's income. The second number ($500 billion) is a measure of how much *future* agreements will add to American incomes. These numbers have been cited widely, spanning the ideological spectrum from the Bush administration to the center-left Hamilton Project of the Brookings Institution.

"Today, U.S. annual incomes are $1 trillion higher, or $9,000 per household, due to increased trade liberalization since 1945."
—Home page of the United States Trade Representative

"…elimination of remaining global barriers [to trade flows] would add another $500 billion to annual income or $4,500 per U.S. household."
— Testimony of the U.S. Trade Representative to the Senate Finance Committee, February 15, 2007

"International trade has generated substantial benefits for the country; estimates suggest that it creates annual benefits amounting to roughly $1 trillion."
— Peter Orzsag, director of the Hamilton Project (Orzsag 2006)

Both numbers are derived from a 2004 study by Bradford, Grieco, and Huf-bauer (BGH, henceforth), published by the Peterson Institute for International Economics. BGH base their findings on a review of a number of independent studies.

The underlying studies upon which the first (retrospective) number is based are of varying quality (from decent to excellent), but *not a single one* argues for benefits to the United States in anything close to the range expressed by BGH. Many of the studies are, in fact, not even attempting to measure the gains from trade liberalization. BGH give the impression that a large number of separate studies came to strikingly common conclusions, lending robustness to the central finding. It's not so—BGH's *reading* of these studies came to a strikingly similar conclusion. This reading is consistently, and extraordinarily, generous to the case that trade liberalization significantly spurs large income gains.

The second (prospective) number is based on a smaller range of studies. BGH again consistently take the maximal position in interpreting what these studies say about the gains from trade liberalization. Further, many of the underlying studies suffer from a major common problem: they assume benefits from removing barriers to trade *even when no existing barrier to trade can be identified.*

This appendix (largely based on an earlier working paper) will lay out, in some detail, reasons to be skeptical of the BGH claims of enormous gains from past and future trade agreements. It will review many of the studies cited by BGH as lending support to the their claim and argue that the $1 trillion and $500 billion numbers are interpretations of these studies that are exceedingly generous to the cause of signing more trade agreements. Lastly, it will point out that the *costs* of expanded trade are radically understated by BGH.

What does economics tell us in general about the gains from trade? Small net gains and large gross losses

The two estimates referenced above are hugely provocative in their characterization of the economics of globalization and demand a skeptical response. First, they are well outside the bounds of what mainstream economics would argue are the straightforward benefits from trade liberalization. Given this, it is incumbent upon BGH to show why previous studies have been so wrong about the benefits of liberalization.

Second, they are based on an "everything and the kitchen sink" approach to thinking about the benefits of trade, larding up every possible channel through which trade liberalization could plausibly improve welfare and assuming that each channel is purely additive with respect to the others. For example, one study reviewed by BGH argues simultaneously that existing price differences between similar goods (say, varieties of T-shirts) are evidence that these goods are *noncompeting* and hence provide benefits through increased variety. However, a separate study argues that existing price differences between similar goods (say, varieties of T-shirts) are evidence that future liberalization-induced competition can close these price differences and provide huge benefits. Surely both of these arguments cannot be true. Either the price differences themselves are evidence of benefits today, or closing them in the future will provide benefits tomorrow, but surely these are not additive.

Third, many of the benefits identified (and the lion's share of *prospective* benefits) depend on assuming that large policy barriers to trade flows exist *even when they cannot be identified*. Observed price differences between commodities or between countries are often chalked up as resulting from *de facto* barriers to trade even when the specific barrier cannot be identified. Many things besides trade policy can result in price differences, and putting concrete numbers on the benefits of removing trade barriers would seem to require *actually identifying the barriers*.

Perhaps more important for those who take trade theory seriously, the BGH characterization of that group losing from expanded trade (concentrated) and the scale of losses (small) is *literally the opposite* of what is implied by mainstream trade theory for an economy like the United States.

As the rest of this book points out, trade theory argues strongly that the outcome of a labor-scarce U.S. economy integrating with a labor-abundant global economy is lower wages for *most* workers in the American economy, period. That is, it is the losses that are quite diffuse (accruing to the majority of the American workforce), while the winnings are concentrated among the minority.

There is one last important issue to highlight regarding the distributional consequences of trade. Mainstream trade theory predicts that the larger the national gains reaped from rich/poor trade, the larger the re-distribution of income and the larger the *gross* losses suffered by the (majority) losing group. Even worse, this theory predicts that more income will be redistributed than created because of trade (one aspect of the so-called "magnification effect"). Given this, it is hugely inaccurate to refer to the losses spurred by trade as either small or concentrated. Further, the larger the gains from trade, the worse the losses suffered by most American workers.

Inflating the gains from trade to assuage the fears of those who face potential harm from globalization is, then, a very odd political strategy. It's like the old joke about a business that loses money on each unit it ships, but plans to "make it up in volume."

Economic theory and calculating gains from liberalization

The less relevant of the two numbers for today's policy debates is the $1 trillion that BGH claim past trade agreements have added to U.S. income. The true degree of its irrelevance can be found in the baseline against which they measure progress on liberalization: the Smoot-Hawley tariff. Nobody in today's political debates is calling for a return to Smoot-Hawley. That said, even their characterization of the gains of moving from Smoot-Hawley levels of protection to today's all-but-tariff-free U.S. economy is out of line with what standard trade theory would predict.

What follows is a quick calculation of the gains from trade using the staid old theory of (static) comparative advantage. It should be noted that, however staid, this is the theory that forms the intellectual foundation for economists' case that trade liberalization is always win-win (again, at the country level).

BGH argue that between the passage of Smoot-Hawley and today the average tariff rate in the United States fell from roughly 40% to less than 2%.[30] We can use a 40% tariff cut to see what this implies for U.S. income growth, using a totally standard method for calculating the gains from trade.

A 40% tariff translates into a 28.5% increase in import prices (derived as $(t/(1+t)$, where t is the tariff rate).

With a 28.5% tariff markup, some goods will be produced domestically even though they could have been produced for 28.5% less abroad. Some goods, however, will be produced domestically but would only be 1% cheaper from abroad. Taking the midpoint, assume a decline in the price of imports of 14.5% over the period in question.

Next, one needs to know the volume of imports that were displaced because of existing tariffs at each moment in time. To do this, one must choose a parameter for the *elasticity of imports with respect to tariff cuts*—this is a measure of the responsiveness of import flows to tariff changes. A generous (for the BGH case) estimate for this parameter is 3. A serious account would figure out the degree of import displacement year-by-year, but again the generous treatment to the BGH case of using the average share of imports in U.S. GDP over the entire period will be used. This counts as generous treatment because the largest tariff reductions occurred when the import share was actually very low, and hence would have provided small benefits.

Since 1970, the average tariff rate has fallen very slowly, while the import share in GDP has risen rapidly. The average import share over the 1947-2005 timespan was 8.3%.

This allows one to calculate the change in imports (measured as a share of GDP) following a tariff cut: multiply the share of imports in GDP (8.3%) by the tariff cut (28.5%) by the elasticity of import response to tariff cuts (3). This gives us a 7.1% increase in imports scaled as a share of GDP.

Multiplying this bloc of imports encouraged by liberalization with the average decline in import prices (14.5%) gives us the cost of this trade protection: 1% of GDP, or well under a quarter of the BGH estimates. This, to be sure, is serious money, and it is obviously a good thing that the U.S. economy no longer has the Smoot-Hawley tariff in place. That said, it's nowhere near the BGH estimates.

If the above example does not convince, perhaps an appeal to authority will. Douglas Irwin, an economic historian who is an expert on American trade policy (and who has written a popular book that is an impassioned *advocacy* for trade liberalization) has examined U.S. trade barriers back to the Civil War. Irwin finds that the GDP costs of these barriers *peaked before 1900* at roughly 1% of GDP, when average tariffs were roughly twice as high as under Smoot-Hawley (the BGH baseline).

Globalization or liberalization?

There's a very important thing to keep in mind here: BGH are not arguing about the benefits of *expanded trade*, or *globalization writ large*. These benefits are surely quite large, larger than those just calculated or measured by Irwin (2007). Their costs are large, too, but leave that aside for a moment.

Instead, BGH are arguing about the benefits of trade *liberalization*, using the policy lever of reducing domestic barriers to foreign commerce. This is a much more restricted ground, especially going forward, as the United States has largely dismantled most serious barriers to foreign commerce. Could *globalization writ large* have added $10,000 to each U.S. household in 2005? Maybe (it's a big claim). *Trade liberalization* absolutely has not.

The tooth fairy

BGH invoke a number of nontraditional channels through which trade can raise incomes (for example, by assuming economies of scale), and this is how they argue for the reasonableness of their estimates in the face of their discordance with standard economic theory. As soon as one introduces influences like scale economies, however, the unambiguously positive result that trade liberalization is always the optimal policy is lost. After all, scale economies could well argue that strategic trade policy that locks in a competitive edge vis-à-vis foreign competitors can be justified. Such considerations, derived from the New Trade Economics of the 1980s, spawned a whole debate on such strategic trade policies in the not-so-distant past.

As just one example of how nontraditional theories do not universally argue for trade liberalization, take the case of commercial aircraft. Scale economies dictate that the global economy will have very few producers of commercial aircraft. These scale economies, combined with history and contingency, led to the United States having the dominant position in commercial aircraft for much of the postwar period. There are reasons to think that the *de facto* national monopoly the United States enjoyed in commercial aircraft was a benefit to the U.S. economy— enough reasons, in fact, to spur European governments to create (and subsidize) a competitor (Airbus). The success of Airbus in terms of a cost/benefit analysis for Europe remains contested. What does not is that the creation of Airbus reduced the monopoly benefits accruing to the U.S. economy from being the only national producer of commercial aircraft.

In a (somewhat related) discussion about the benefits of liberalization of international financial (as opposed to goods) markets, economist Brad DeLong has referred to the willingness to bring in speculative hypotheses from outside the core of accepted economic theory as "invoking the tooth fairy." This was not said pejoratively—sometimes the tooth fairy has valuable things to say, and all branches of economics should strive to recognize good insights that are not currently enshrined in the textbook. That said, it is far from clear that in the trade debate the tooth fairy uniformly recommends liberalization; plenty of alternative theories would argue for greater *costs* (not benefits) stemming from liberalization than are currently recognized. BGH seem to characterize all possible channels through which trade could possibly impact an economy as necessarily positive for the case for liberalization. This just is not so.

Notes on specific studies

This section has some detailed remarks on many of the studies surveyed in BGH. The large number of studies surveyed by BGH is implicitly invoked by them as arguing for a robustness check on their central findings. As we will see, these studies really do not converge on anything like an argument that past trade agreements have added $1 trillion to the U.S. economy.

OECD (2003)

The first study referenced by BGH is OECD (2003). It uses the trade share of overall GDP as an explanatory variable in a growth regression based on a panel of OECD countries. This is an inadequate and potentially misleading way to measure the impact of trade on growth, for a couple of reasons.[31] First, the *causality* is far from clear between trade and growth. Indeed, trade theory has much more to say definitively about the impact of growth on trade flows than the reverse.

Second, the trade share of GDP is an almost wholly uninformative measure of a nation's *policy* stance. The openness of Vietnam measured with this metric is 300% higher than that of the United States. Yet nobody would seriously argue that Vietnam has a much more liberal and open economy in a policy relevant sense than the United States.[32] Third, while BGH cite Cline's (1997) estimates that half of the increase in trade over the relevant time period is driven by falling trade costs, this includes costs that fall due to technology (transport costs) not just policy changes, which is what BGH explicitly claim they are focusing on.

In short, the OECD (2003) study is almost a lesson in how *not* to disentangle the impacts of trade policy on growth. The authors of the study recognize this, writing:

> The possible reverse causality problem in the relationship between trade and economic growth suggests some caution in interpreting empirical results. In particular, we treat the intensity of trade in the growth equation as an indicator of trade exposure—capturing features such as competitive pressures— rather than one with direct policy implications.

Given this, and given the misreading of the Cline (1997) findings on trade costs, it seems that BGH do not use the same caution as the authors of the OECD study in making policy pronouncements about the benefits of liberalization. This pattern continues throughout.

Bernard, Jensen, and Schott (BJS)

A 2003 paper by Bernard, Jensen, and Schott (BJS1, henceforth) is cited by BGH to further justify their claim that trade added $1 trillion in benefits to the U.S. economy. However, the results from BJS1 are from a *simulation*, not an *estimation*. The authors of the original study themselves say, "Because our model is stylized, the particular numbers generated by these counterfactual simulations should be seen as suggestive more than definitive."

BGH cite a related paper (Bernard, Jensen, and Schott (BJS2) 2004) as empirical support for their reading of the BJS1 results. BJS2 estimate the effect of falling trade costs (either policy or technology driven) on productivity growth in manufacturing firms. One regression specification from BJS2 finds a 1% fall in trade costs results in a 1% increase in productivity. The channel for this productivity improvement (this becomes important later) is the displacement of lower-productivity domestic firms by imports.

BGH essentially take the 40% tariff they posit as characterizing the 1947 U.S. economy and argue that manufacturing productivity is 40% higher today because of trade agreements signed in the past, which translates into roughly $600 billion in trade benefits.

A careful reading of BJS2, however, argues that this is not a proper interpretation of their results. BJS2 do not even find a statistically significant effect of falling trade costs on manufacturing productivity in the aggregate. Instead, they find this relationship in a sample restricted to trade with OECD countries within industries characterized by high levels of intra-industry trade—a sample that includes 65 out of a possible 450 industries.

In short, this sort of productivity-enhancing effects of falling trade barriers seems to characterize only trade with rich nations in industries with lots of intra-industry trade. This is an interesting and important finding, but it cannot be applied to the total manufacturing sector.

Lastly, it's worth noting that, since most of the heavy lifting in trade liberalization was done early on (since they are measuring from Smoot-Hawley peaks), BGH end up showing that the BJS channels suggest that trade liberalization has added all of $9 (yes, *nine dollars*) per U.S. household from 1982 to the present (see table 2.4 in BGH). Post-1982 is, remember, the era that saw the completion of the Uruguay Round of the General Agreement on Tariffs and Trade (GATT, which saw perhaps the most wide-ranging global commitment to liberalization of any of the GATT rounds), formation of the World Trade Organization (WTO, which replaced GATT), the passage of the North American Free Trade Agreement

(NAFTA), along with many other bilateral agreements, the permanent normalization of trading relations with China, and China's entry into the WTO. In short, when people today argue about globalization, they are arguing essentially about the post-1982 period.

Broda and Weinstein (2003)

BGH next cite Broda and Weinstein (BW, henceforth), who argue that large benefits of trade liberalization come through *product variety* and cite as evidence continuing price differentials even within finely disaggregated industrial classifications (T-shirts, say). These price differences are taken by BW as evidence that these goods are actually noncompeting and serve to boost welfare by providing greater choice to consumers.

The BW study is high quality and quite convincing as to trade providing gains through variety. The problem with BGH's treatment of its findings, however, is that they simply add the implied benefits from variety effects directly to other findings—including the BJS findings on competition-induced productivity effects.

This, of course, raises an important question of interpretation. BJS1&2 posit that increasing global competition causes less-productive domestic firms to wither and die while more-productive domestic firms scale up production. This reallocation effect boosts productivity.

However, if imports are largely adding to variety and often do not directly compete with domestically produced output (a la BW), then one must ask why they are killing domestic plants and leading to productivity enhancement through the allocation effects identified by BJS. Simply adding these two benefits together seems odd.

Bradford and Lawrence (BL)

This same issue of interpreting simulation results as empirical findings clouds the results from Bradford and Lawrence (BL) (2004b). BGH report results from this paper as supportive of their large number on the gains from trade. However, the BL (2004b) results stem from a simulation performed on a computable general equilibrium (CGE) model. CGE models are commonly used in trade policy, and the outcomes of each particular model hinge significantly (that is, entirely) on the assumptions underlying the structure of the model. For example, BL (2004b) assume in their model that there are economies of scale in production. This adds to the gains from trade, as globalization allows producers to spread large production runs over more consumers. However, it is far from clear that this is the proper assumption; many other CGE models assume constant (not increasing) returns to scale. Further, it is (again) far from clear that economies of scale always imply gains from trade liberalization, especially for a large country like the United States, where the domestic market (the world's largest) provides plenty of room for domestic industries to realize most conceivable benefits from scale. Lastly, gains from trade stemming from economies of scale necessarily come at the expense of gains from trade coming through variety.

Economies of scale allow firms to spread production runs over very large consumer markets, but utility gains from consuming a wide array of goods work directly against the benefits of scale in production. As Taylor and Ocampo (1997) have succinctly put it:

> It makes little sense to introduce one more yuppie automobile marque if its intended consumers' preferences for diversity are going to limit sales to an uneconomical 100,000 units per year.

Again, a judgment on which effect dominates or the degree to which there is tension among the different channels through which trade affects the domestic economy would have been useful. Instead, the gains are stacked on top of each other, and the authors move on to another piece.

While the full set of BL (2004b) assumptions are not identified in BGH, it is worth noting at least an issue that seems to plague most CGE models of trade policy. Tariffs are a tax and, like all taxes, cause economic distortions that can reduce potential output. CGE models of trade policy calibrate what economic output would be in the absence of this tax. Since, however, governments in the real world would need to find a way to reclaim some of the revenue foregone by tariff cuts, the CGE models need to specify how non-tariff taxes are raised. Almost across the board, CGE models assume that "lump-sum taxes" replace the tariff. A lump sum tax is a tax of a fixed amount that has to be paid by everyone regardless of the level of his or her income. Lump sum taxes are considered more efficient than almost all other taxes because they do not influence a person's decision on how much to work. The problem, however, is that lump-sum taxes do not exist anywhere in the real world. In essence, some of the gains from trade embedded in trade policy CGE models rest in the fact that a real-world tax (tariffs) is assumed to be replaced by a theoretically optimal tax that doesn't actually exist anywhere in the real world (lump-sum taxes). This surely overstates the gains from trade.

Richardson (2004)

In an appendix, BGH use work sourced to Richardson (2004, unpublished) to further bolster the $1 trillion number. They undertake an *aggregate* growth accounting exercise that finds that a rising share of imported intermediate inputs per worker has led to a massive increase in aggregate productivity.

This literally cannot be true: *aggregate* growth accounting does not count the influence of inputs, period, imported or otherwise. Inputs are subtracted out of all output measures to yield value-added, the relevant metric here. This is a truly odd mistake to make.

At the industry level, input-deepening *can*, by itself, raise productivity. However, this deepening only results in higher *aggregate* productivity if the reallocation of inputs from one industry to another results in more efficient production. For example, if some activities are outsourced from one sector to another (say GM firing its own janitors and hiring a cleaning service from the business services sector), and if the new provider of inputs is more efficient (the cleaning service can raise cleaning productivity), then productivity gains will show up in the "reallocation effects" that are calculated. But simple input-deepening—using more inputs per unit of gross output—cannot raise aggregate productivity.

In short, this appendix is utterly silent on the issue of past gains from trade.

$500 billion in future benefits?

Some more forward-looking advocates of signing more trade agreements have pointed to the prospective gains identified in BGH (2004).

These prospective gains have been criticized earlier in Bivens (2007), but some of those criticisms will be repeated here.

Again, what does theory say?

As before, we can quickly generate the estimate of what future liberalizations should add to U.S. incomes based on traditional (static) trade theory. The United States today has an average tariff rate of less than 2%. This low *average* rate may mask some higher peak tariffs on particular goods and non-tariff barriers that keep imports out the country. Say (generously to the case for trade liberalization) that the *effective* tariff rate into the U.S. economy is five times as large as the simple average—the equivalent of a 10% tariff on all imports (most estimates of the *effective* rate of protection are actually only around twice as high as the *average* rate).

Using the same exercise performed earlier in the paper about the effects of removing a 40% tariff, one can pretty easily calculate what removing all of these trade barriers would imply for U.S. income. Unsurprisingly, even the most generous assumptions yield the result that removing a 10% tariff barrier would add about 0.26% to GDP, or roughly $30 billion. This is a high-end estimate of what can be banked. The other $470 billion-ish cited by BGH needs a lot of explaining.

It should also be noted here that it is a little odd to claim $1 trillion in benefits in going from 40% Smoot-Hawley tariffs to less than 10% tariffs, but then claim that going from 10% to zero will still add another $500 billion in benefits. The marginal costs of each 1% in tariff levels are actually supposed to *shrink*, not increase, the closer they get to zero.

Where does the $500 billion number come from?

BGH essentially invoke three studies to justify the $500 billion estimate of *prospective* gains from liberalization. The first one was a 2001 study by Brown, Deardorff, and Stern (BDS, henceforth) using the Michigan Model of World Production and Trade. The second is a 2004 study by Bradford and Lawrence (BL, henceforth). Results from both studies regarding the gains from trade can be described (uncharitably, perhaps, but largely accurately) as premised overwhelmingly on the assumption that barriers to trade exist *even when no explicit price or quantity restrictions on imports or foreign investment can be identified.*

The third study uses a finding by Rose (2003), in a paper generally unrelated to the issue of gains from trade, and applies its findings to coefficients derived from the OECD (2003) study referenced above.

Brown, Deardorff, and Stern (BDS)

For example, BDS estimate that about 85% of projected U.S. gains from future trade liberalizations will come from liberalization of the service sector. This will surprise many, since it's not common to think of the U.S. service sector as benefiting greatly from trade protection. However, BDS use a very expansive definition of protection to get their results.

Essentially, they look at *gross operating margins* across industries and countries. As a baseline, they take the lowest gross operating margin that exists in any country for each particular industry, and from there they assume that the difference between this and operating margins in the same industry located in other countries is *solely the result of a policy barrier to trade that can be removed.*

This method yields the hard-to-believe result that the service sector in the United States is notably inefficient and protected relative to the rest of the world, as gross operating margins are higher in three of four categories in the United States relative to the rest of the world.

Dornan (2001) notes that BDS cite Hoekman (2000) as the source for this methodological approach. However, Hoekman (2000) actually cites this approach as just one of many. Another method used by Hoekman (2000) is to identify *actual trade barriers* and weight them according to interviews with selected businesses that work in the protected areas.

Using this approach, the United States is far and away the *least* protected service market identified, not more restrictive than the average, which the BDS results suggest (unlike the gross margin numbers, in the qualitative ranking, a lower number implies greater openness and less protection). This second approach implies very little gain to the United States from further liberalizing its service sector, as access to it is already as free as the global economy allows anywhere.

Further, as noted in this context by Baker and Weisbrot (2002), it's a general fact that even different firms within the same industry in a given country often have very different gross operating margins—Safeway's margin (29%) is over 50% higher than its industry average (18%). Target's margin is 50% greater than Wal-Mart's, yet very few people think there are explicit policy barriers to Target competing with Wal-Mart within the United States.

BDS acknowledge that their method does not provide an airtight estimate of the trade barriers faced by service-sector firms, allowing that "these estimates of services barriers are intended to be indirect approximations of what the actual barriers may in fact be" (p. 18).

When the World Bank (2002) adopted a similar approach to forecasting gains from service trade, it noted "the quantification of services sectors' trade barriers and other forms of protection is still more art than science" (World Bank 2002, 170).

Art has its place. But it's not in ginning up huge numbers to throw around in policy debates that should be largely based on numbers that we know about, not those we imagine we see in the gaps.

Bradford and Lawrence (BL)

The BL study takes price differences between commodities classified similarly (T-shirts, say) as evidence of barriers to trade that should erode these differences, again without actually pointing to identifiable trade barriers.

Further, while the BL study does not examine the service sector, BGH "scale up" the BL results on merchandise trade by looking at the ratio of service sector to merchandise liberalization benefits identified by BDS. What looks to be a robust result (two studies converging on a common number for what future trade agreements can bring the U.S. economy) turns out to hinge in large measure on how convincing only one of the studies is.

Rose (2003)

Lastly, BGH point to a study by Andrew Rose (2003) on the effect of signing trade agreements on the volume of trade conducted in a nation. Rose, it should be noted, finds very little impact of multilateral trade agreements (joining the World Trade Organization, for example) on the volume of trade. He does, however, find that signing regional trade agreements (RTAs, an example being NAFTA) increases the volume of bilateral trade between nations.

BGH take a finding from Rose that signing an RTA increases bilateral trade by 118% between nations, and apply it to an assumption of what would happen if "RTAs were concluded with all [U.S.] trading partners." They make an adjustment (knocking off 25% of the coefficient) to reflect that some of the increase in trade that occurs with the signing of RTAs reflects trade diversion, not a net increase in trade.

This leaves, however, the strange result that somehow one form of liberalization (RTAs) leads to trading increases, yet another form of liberalization (arguably more comprehensive and ambitious multilateral agreements like the WTO) does not.

This is a genuine puzzle, and it seems odd to argue that one finding can be applied to a hypothetical world of comprehensive liberalization while the other can be thrown in the waste bin. This seems especially inappropriate given that there is a well-known concern about interpreting simple correlations between existing RTAs and high volumes of bilateral trade: often countries that already conduct lots of bilateral trade are more likely to sign RTAs (this is called the "natural trading partner" effect). In short, the judgment that a weight of 100% should be given to Rose's RTA coefficient and 0% to his findings on multilateral trade institutions seems too generous to the argument that liberalization increases trade flows.

Thinking for a second what this argues, BGH seem to be implying that the United States should be working not for multilateral global liberalization through the WTO, but rather should try to encourage each country in the world to sign bilateral free trade agreements (FTAs) with each and every other country in the world. This is not fleshed out in their study.

Setting this aside for a moment, BGH apply the Rose finding and argue that a series of thousands of global bilateral FTAs would increase trade between the United States and all its trading partners by 60%. They then grab the coefficient from the OECD (2003) study referenced earlier and argue that this translates into a $1.3 trillion increase in GDP for the United States.

Again, however, what looks to be a robustness check of several different studies converging on relatively common outcomes turns out to depend crucially on how reliable one finds a much smaller number of underlying studies: if one does not find the OECD (2003) finding convincing, then the BGH reading of Rose will be similarly unconvincing.

Conclusion

Flatly said, past trade liberalization has not add $9,000 per U.S. household, and future liberalization will not add $4,500. These numbers come from a consistently too-generous reading of a small subsample of the literature on the gains from trade liberalization and from imagining trade barriers that have not been proved to actually exist.

Generally in trade debates it can be safely stipulated (even by those concerned about the impact of globalization on working Americans) that economic theory predicts that removal of trade barriers leads to higher national incomes. This can be stipulated because it is true, because the optimal progressive response to the long-run problems posed by globalization to American workers does not include trade protection, and because it helps move the debate along to more contested areas (who gets the net benefits generated by liberalization).

However, these numbers are clearly meant to intimidate those who express any concern about the impacts of our current policy stance regarding globalization. The truth is that slowing down the pace of global integration will have imperceptible impacts on American living standards, and there just is not $4,500 per family at stake in making sure that, say, CAFTA and the Peru FTA are not held up by Congress.

There's an honest and rigorous case to be made about why the United States should keep barriers to foreign commerce open. There's an honest and rigorous case to be made why such policies demand some recompense for those who are harmed by them. BGH's numbers do not fit in this debate, and should be retired from public discussion.

APPENDIX 5

The multivariate regressions shown here in **Tables A5-1** and **A5-2** confirm the statistical significance of the trendlines in Figures 3B and 3C in Chapter 3.

TABLE A5-1. Regression analysis of Figure 3-A:
Changes in labor intensity and LDC import share across industries

	1	2	3	4	5	6
LDC import share	-0.33**	-0.32***	-0.27***	-0.61***	-0.60***	-0.52***
	[3.52]	[3.48]	[2.92]	[4.85]	[4.79]	[4.24]
Output		-0.0116**	-0.0117**		0.0086	0.0002
		[2.26]	[2.33]		[1.29]	[0.02]
K/Y ratio			0.0358***			0.0486***
			[5.30]			[4.77]
Constant	-0.2646***	-0.2119***	-0.1731***	-0.1103***	-0.1461***	-0.1357***
	[9.95]	[6.00]	[4.88]	[2.67]	[2.94]	[2.81]
Timespan	Full sample	Full sample	Full sample	1989-2002	1989-2002	1989-2002
Observations	806	806	806	367	367	367
R-squared	0.0151	0.0214	0.0545	0.0604	0.0647	0.1199

Note: Dependent variable is the change in production workers' share of industry wage-bill.
Absolute value of t statistics in brackets.
* Significant at 10% level; ** significant at 5%; *** significant at 1%.

Source: Author's analysis of data from the NBER Productivity Database and the Census Bureau.

TABLE A5-2. Regression analysis of Figure 3-C:
Price changes and labor intensity across industries

	1	2	3	4
Production worker share	-0.6	-1.05	-0.75	-1.04
	[1.45]	[2.69]***	[1.41]	[2.07]**
TFP		-0.77		-0.91
		[9.80]***		[9.98]***
Constant	3.39	3.12	3.2	2.95
	[29.75]***	[28.19]***	[21.81]***	[21.06]***
Weights	no	no	yes	yes
Observations	283	283	283	283
R-squared	0.028	0.1176	0.027	0.1212
Observations	806	806	806	367
R-squared	0.0151	0.0214	0.0545	0.0604

Note: Dependent variable is percent change in industry value-added price between 1989 and 2002.
Absolute value of t statistics in brackets.
* Significant at 10% level; ** significant at 5%; *** significant at 1%.

Source: Author's analysis of data from the NBER Productivity Database and the Census Bureau.

ENDNOTES

1   A small wage insurance pilot program now exists under TAA.

2   See Delong and Cohen (2005) and Blinder (2007).

3   This book focuses largely on the trade account, leaving immigration and capital flows to the side. This focus, however, makes its estimates of the distributional impacts of globalization essentially a lower bound, as it is widely considered that immigration flows and capital mobility also contribute to growing inequality.

4   This is not to say that such trade is always and everywhere costless. Chapter 3 discusses some theories of how even rich/rich trade can have adverse effects on large subgroups of American workers. That said, the bulk of this book, and the bulk of the economic literature in general, focuses on the distributional consequences of rich/poor trade as the main threat globalization poses to the living standards across the American workforce.

5   See Dew-Becker and Gordon (2007).

6   It is possible that gains in total compensation (wages plus benefits) for this group will match up better with productivity, but it seems unlikely, as wage gains and total compensation gains tend not to diverge too dramatically over time, which makes sense since wages are almost 80% of total compensation on average.

7   An example is *proprietors' income,* which refers to income earned by noncorporate businesses. Given that many of these businesses are quite small, it's far from obvious whether or not such income should be classified as accruing to "labor" or "capital." To get around this issue, economists commonly examine the distribution of labor and capital incomes in the corporate sector (about 75% of all private sector income), where all income is classified as either one or the other.

8   As has been noted by many (perhaps most forcefully in recent work by Chang (2002)), this is essentially a static argument that does not allow for, say, the secretary to gain skills and get better at legal services over time if she trains. It is therefore true that the economic policy relevance of comparative advantage is much more limited than is generally recognized by the elite policy-making community. That said, it remains a powerful argument in its own right and should not be ignored by those seeking to understand globalization.

9   In versions with more than two goods, this should be modified with the clause "for any reasonable weight of imports in final demand by U.S. consumers."

10 The appendix draws heavily on Deardorff (1993). Cline (1997) provides the best wall-to-wall coverage of the academic trade and wages debate.

11 If this sounds unrealistic, remember that this is a story about what matters over a reasonably long period of time. While people obviously do not lose an apparel job on Monday and begin working at Boeing on Tuesday, in the relatively fluid American economy people do switch across many economic sectors throughout their working lives.

12 See the appendix for the algebraic derivation of the "magnification effects."

13 Rodrik (1994), noting the consequences of this magnification effect, has labeled the redistributive effects of liberalization the "first-order" (i.e., most important) effects.

14 The key word here is "extreme." Belief that both trade and immigration can affect United States wages is perfectly compatible with all but the most extreme forms of the FPET.

15 For more on this recent literature, see Appendix 1D. The main exemplars of it are Davis and Weinstein (2001, 2003a, 2003b), and this work informs my updates of FCA later in the chapter.

16 Most notably Davis (1995), Davis and Weinstein (2003a, 2003b), and Schott (2003).

17 For a little more detail on specific studies, see Appendix 1.

18   A model of intermediate complexity (and results) is Harrigan (2000), which is discussed in Appendix 1F.

19   See Appendix 1G for a more complete explanation.

20   Respectively, these studies are Wood (1994) and Feenstra and Hanson (1995), Feenstra and Hanson (1999), and Cline (1997), for the FCA, PPR, and CGE methodologies.

21   Katz and Murphy (1992) is perhaps most the most well known of the "high" estimates of this elasticity.

22   It should be noted that the Krugman (1995) model doesn't suffer from the assumption of perfect tradeability in the economy. By scaling less developed imports against total U.S. GDP and making this variable the centerpiece of the model, Krugman is implicitly accounting for the relative importance of traded goods. The 1223 model improves on the Krugman model only in allowing other determinants of relative wages (changing supplies of labor and professionals) to be tested alongside trade flows.

23   Freeman, Krugman, and Cline are among the most intelligent authors writing on the subject of trade and wages, and the use of these quotations is meant not to illustrate myopia on their part but rather to show the sea change that has occurred in perceptions about trade's potential impact on the U.S. economy in the era of offshoring.

24   See Appendix 3 for a sampling of these claims.

25   In all cases, I use the most conservative estimate of the elasticity of substitution between labor and skills.

26   The virtues of closing the 75-year actuarial shortfall are deeply contested, as is the size of the gap itself. The view of many experts is that there is no need to close this gap today, tomorrow, or perhaps ever.

27   See Bivens (2006) for a recap of this argument.

28   The cost of a four-year degree is hard to quantify with precision, given the huge variance in college costs. Row 6 takes the simple average of the costs of four years of in-state tuition at a public university. It then shows what a family would have to save each year if it had 18 years to prepare for this cost. The annual average tuition at public four-year universities was almost $5,500 in 2006 (College Board 2007). Applying normal rates of inflation (6% per year for higher education), we'll say that a four-year degree costs $27,000 for families starting in 2007. If they had been saving for 18 years and earned essentially the real rate of return on treasury bills over this time (say 3%), this comes out to roughly $1,100 per year they needed to put away for the degree.

29   Generally, and unexpectedly, high-wage workers in even developing countries seem to have been beneficiaries of globalization as well. Feenstra and Hanson (1995) and Verhoogen (2004) put forward theories as to why. An essential insight of each is that globalization may actually allow all countries to move into more skill-intensive production than what would characterize their autarky output, raising skill demands globally.

30   This is not quite right. It's true that the average tariff imposed by Smoot-Hawley was 40%, but many imports were not affected by Smoot-Hawley. The average tariff rate relative to the total value of U.S. imports was roughly 20%. Lerdau (1957) constructed an annual "effective weighted tariff rate" to get a better gauge of commercial policy restrictiveness, and he finds that Smoot-Hawley peaks were just a shade over 30%. For this paper, the high-end 40% estimate will be used.

31   For exhaustive reasons why, see Rodriguez and Rodrik (2001) and Frankel and Romer (1999).

32   While the OECD study tries to control for one aspect of this difference (country size), there are many other reasons (geography, in particular) as to why one country might see larger trade volumes than another even given the same trade policy regime.

REFERENCES

Anderson, K., W. Martin, and D. Van der Mensbrugghe. 2006. Distortions to world trade: impacts on agricultural markets and farm incomes from full trade liberalization. *Review of Agricultural Economics.* Vol. 28, No. 2, pp. 168–94.

Baker, D., and M. Weisbrot. 2002. "The Relative Impact of Trade Liberalization on Developing Countries." Center for Economic Policy Research Briefing Paper. Washington, D.C.: CEPR.

Baldwin, R.E., and G.G. Cain. 1997. "Shifts in U.S. Relative Wages: The Role of Trade, Technology, and Factor Endowments." Working Paper No. 5934. Cambridge, Mass.: National Bureau of Economic Research.

Bardhan, A., and C. Kroll. 2003. "The Next Wave of Outsourcing." Research Report. University of California, Berkeley: Fisher Center for Real Estate and Urban Economics.

Baumol, W. 2005. "Errors in economics and their consequences. *Social Research.* Vol. 72, No. 1, pp. 1–25.

Bergsten, F. 2006. *America and the World Economy: A Strategy for the Next Decade.* Transcript found at: http://www.cfr.org/ publication/7786/america_and_the_world_economy. html?bre adcrumb=%2Fbios%2F257%2Fpeter_g_peterson

Berman, E., J. Bound, and Z. Griliches. 1994. Changes in the demand for skilled labor within U.S. manufacturing: Evidence from the Annual Survey of Manufactures. *Quarterly Journal of Economics.* May, pp. 367–97.

Bernard, A., and J.B. Jensen. 1997. Exporters, skill upgrading, and the wage gap. *Journal of International Economics.* Vol. 42, pp. 3–31.

Bernard, A.B. and J.B. Jensen. 1998. "Understanding increasing and decreasing wage inequality." Working Paper No. 6571. Cambridge, Mass.: National Bureau of Economic Research.

Bernard, A, J.B. Jensen, and P. Schott. 2003. "Falling trade costs, heterogeneous firms, and industry dynamics." Working Paper No. 03/10. London: Institute for Fiscal Studies.

Bernard, A., and J.B. Jensen. 2004. "Exporting and productivity in the U.S." Tuck School of Business at Dartmouth, National Bureau of Economic Research, and the Institute for International Economics. Photocopy (July).

Bernard, A., S. Redding, and P. Schott. 2004. "Comparative advantage and heterogeneous firms." Working Paper No. 10668. Cambridge, Mass.: National Bureau of Economic Research.

Bhagwati, J., and V. Dehejia. 1994. "Free Trade and the Wages of the Unskilled: Is Marx Striking Again?" In J. Bhagwati and M.H. Kosters, eds., *Trade and Wages: Leveling Wages Down?* Washington, D.C.: AEI Press.

Blinder, A. 2007. "How many U.S. jobs might be offshorable?" Unpublished Working Paper.

Borjas, G., R. Freeman, and L. Katz. 1992. "On the Labor-Market Effects of Immigration and Trade." In G.J. Borjas and Richard Freeman, eds., *Immigration and the Work Force.* Chicago, Ill.: University of Chicago Press.

Borjas, G., R. Freeman, and L. Katz. 1997. How much do immigration and trade affect labor market outcomes? *Brookings Papers on Economic Activity.* Washington, D.C.: Brookings Institution, pp. 1-67.

Borjas, G., and V. Ramey. 1994. Rising wage inequality in the United States: Causes and consequences. *AEA Papers and Proceedings.* Vol. 84, No. 1, pp. 11-22.

Borjas, G. J., and V. A. Ramey. 1995. Foreign competition, market power, and wage inequality. *Quarterly Journal of Economics.* Vol. 110, No. 4, pp. 1110.

Bradford, S., and R. Lawrence. 2004a. *Has Globalization Gone Far Enough? The Costs of Fragmented Markets.* Washington, D.C.: Institute for International Economics.

Bradford, S., and R. Lawrence. 2004b. "Non-MFN CGE Simulations." Brigham Young University and Harvard University. Mimeo.

Brown, D., A. Deardorff, and R. Stern. 2001. "CGE modeling and analysis of multilateral and regional negotiating options." Research Seminar in International Economics Discussion Paper No. 468. Ann Arbor, Mich.: University of Michigan School of Public Policy.

Choi, M. 2003. "Threat effect of foreign direct investment on labor union wage premium." Working Paper No. 27. Amherst, Mass.: Political Economy Research Institute.

Cline, W. 1997. *Trade and Income Distribution.* Washington, D.C.: Institute for International Economics.

College Board. 2007. "Trends in College Pricing." Washington, D.C.: The Coollege Board. www.collegeboard.com/trends

Cooper, R. 1994. "Foreign trade, wages, and unemployment." Cambridge, Mass.: Harvard University.

Davis, D., and D. Weinstein. 2001. An account of global factor trade. *American Economic Review.* Vol. 91, No. 5.

Davis, D. 1998. Does European unemployment prop up American wages? National labor markets and global trade. *American Economic Review.* Vol. 88, No. 3.

Davis, D., and D. Weinstein. 2003a. "The Factor Content of Trade." In J. Choi and J. Harrigan, eds., *The Handbook of International Trade.* London: Blackwell.

Davis, D., and D. Weinstein. 2003b. "Do factor endowments matter for north-north trade?" Working Paper No. 8516. Cambridge, Mass.: National Bureau of Economic Research.

Deardorff, A. 1994. "An Overview of the Stolper-Samuelson Theorem." In A. Deardorff and R.M. Stern, eds., *The Stolper-Samuelson Theorem: A Golden Jubilee.* Ann Arbor, Mich.: University of Michigan Press.

Deardorff, A., and D. Haikura. 1994. "Trade and Wages: What Are the Questions?" In J. Bhagwati and M. Kosters, eds., *Trade and Wages: Leveling Wages Down.* Washington, D.C.: AEI Press.

DeLong, J.B., and S. Cohen. 2005. Shaken and stirred. *Atlantic.* January/February.

Dimaranan, B., T. Hertel, and W. Martin. 2002. "Potential Gains From Post-Uruguay Round Trade Reform: Impacts on Developing Countries." In A. McCalla and J. Nash, eds., *Reforming Agricultural Trade for Developing Countries: Quantifying the Impacts of Multilateral Trade Reform.* Washington, D.C.: World Bank.

Dinopolous, E., and P. Segerstrom. 1999. A Schumpeterian model of protection and relative wages. *American Economic Review.* Vol. 89, No. 3, pp. 450-72.

Dornan, P. 2001. "The free trade magic act." Briefing Paper. Washington, D.C.: Economic Policy Institute.

Ethier, Wilfred J. 1984. Protection and real incomes once again. *Quarterly Journal of Economics.* Vol. 99, No. 1, pp. 193-200.

Feenstra, R. C., and G. Hanson. 1995. "Foreign Investment, Outsourcing, and Relative Wages." In R.C. Feenstra and Gene M. Grossman, eds., *Political Economy of Trade Policy: Essays in Honor of Jagdish Bhagwati.* Cambridge, Mass.: MIT Press.

Feenstra, R. C., and G. Hanson. 1996. Globalization, outsourcing, and wage inequality. *American Economic Review.* pp. 240-45.

Feenstra, R. C., and G. Hanson. 1999. Productivity measurement and the impact of trade and technology on wages: Estimates for the U.S., 1972-1990. *Quarterly Journal of Economics.* August, pp. 907-40.

Feenstra, R., G. Hanson, and D. Swenson. 2000. "Offshore Assembly From the United States: Production Characteristics of the 9802 Program." In Robert C. Feenstra, ed., *The Impact of International Trade on Wages.* University of Chicago Press and the National Bureau of Economic Research, pp. 85-128.

Feenstra, R., and C. Shiells. 1997. "Bias in U.S. Import Prices and Demand." In Timothy Bresnahan and Robert Gordon, eds., *New Products: History, Methodology, and Applications.* University of Chicago Press and the National Bureau of Economic Research, pp. 249-76.

Forrester Research. 2004. "3.3 Million U.S. Services Jobs To Go Offshore." Research Brief. Cambridge, Mass.: Forrester Research.

Frankel, J., and D. Romer. 1999. Trade and growth: An empirical investigation. *American Economic Review.* Vol. 89, No. 3, pp. 379–99.

Freeman, R.B. 1995. Are your wages set in Beijing? *Journal of Economic Perspectives.* Vol. 9, No. 3, pp. 15-32.

Goldberg, L., and J. Tracy. 2001. "Exchange rates and wages." Working Paper No. W8137. Cambridge, Mass.: National Bureau of Economic Research.

Harrigan, James. 2000. "International Trade and American Wages in General Equilibrium, 1967-1995." In Robert C. Feenstra, ed., *The Impact of International Trade on Wages.* Chicago, Ill.: University of Chicago Press.

Hoekman, B. 2000. The next round of services negotiations: identifying priorities and options. *Federal Reserve Bank of St. Louis Review.* Vol. 82, pp. 31-47.

Irwin, D. 2007. "Trade restrictiveness and deadweight losses from U.S. tariffs." Working Paper No. 13450. Cambridge, Mass.: National Bureau of Economic Research.

Jensen, J.B., and L. Kletzer. 2005. "Tradable Services: Understanding the Scope and Impact of Services Offshoring." In Lael Brainard and Susan M. Collins, eds., *Brookings Trade Forum 2005: Offshoring White-Collar Work—The Issues and the Implications.* Forthcoming.

Katz, L.F., and K.M. Murphy. 1992. Changes in relative wages, 1963-1987: supply and demand factors. *Quarterly Journal of Economics.* Vol. 107, pp. 35-78.

Kirkegaard, J. 2004. "Outsourcing: Stains on the white collar?" Washington, D.C.: Institute for International Economics. Available at http://www.iie.com/publications/papers/kirkegaard0204.pdf

Krugman, P. 1995. Growing world trade: causes and consequences. *Brookings Papers on Economic Activity.* Vol. 1, pp. 327-77.

Krugman, P. 1996. Review of William Grieder, *One World, Ready or Not: The Manic Logic of Global Capitalism. Washington Post Book World.* Available at http://web.mit.edu/krugman/www/greider.html

Krugman, P. 2000. Technology, trade, and factor prices. *Journal of International Economics.* Vol. 50, No. 1, pp. 51-71.

Krugman, P., and M. Obstfeld. 1994. *International Economics: Theory and Policy.* 3rd Edition. New York, N.Y.: Harper-Collins.

Krueger, A.B. 1997. "Labor market shifts and the price puzzle revisited." Working Paper. Cambridge, Mass.: National Bureau of Economic Research.

Lawrence, R.Z., and M.J. Slaughter. 1993. "International Trade and American Wages in the 1980s: Giant Sucking Sound or Small Hiccup?" *Brookings Papers on Economic Activity: Microeconomics 2,* pp. 161-211.

Leamer, E.E. 1993. "U.S. Wages and the Mexican-U.S. Free Trade Agreement." In Peter Garber, ed., *The Mexico- U.S. Free Trade Agreement.* Cambridge, Mass.: MIT Press, pp. 57-128.

Leamer, E.E. 1998. "In Search of Stolper-Samuelson Linkages Between International Trade and Lower Wages." In S. Collins, ed., *Imports, Exports, and the American Worker.* Washington, D.C.: Brookings Institution.

Leamer, E.E. 2000. What's the use of factor contents? *Journal of International Economics.* Vol. 50, pp. 17-49.

Lovely, M.E., and J.D. Richardson. 1998. "Trade flows and wage premiums: Does who or what matter?" Working Paper No. W6668. Cambridge, Mass.: National Bureau of Economic Research.

Mallaby, Sebastian. 2007. Free trade: pause or fast-forward. *Washington Post.* March 2.

Mincer, J. 1991. "Human Capital, Technology, and the Wage Structure: What Do Time Series Show?" Working Paper No. 3581. Cambridge, Mass.: National Bureau of Economic Research.

Murphy, K.M., and F. Welch. 1993. The structure of wages. *Quarterly Journal of Economics.* Vol. 107, February, pp. 285-326.

Ocampo, J.A., and L. Taylor. 1998. Trade liberalization in developing economies: modest benefits but problems with pProductivity growth, macro prices, and income distribution. *Economic Journal.* Vol. 108, pp. 1523-46.

Organization for Economic Cooperation and Development. 2003. *The Sources of Economic Growth in OECD Countries.* Paris: OECD.

Orzsag, Peter. 2006. "Warm hearts and cool heads: promoting growth and oppportunity in a globalizing economy." Remarks at the APEC Symposium on Socio-Economic Disparity, Seoul, South Korea, June 29.

Richardson, J.D. 2004. "'Sizing up' the micro-data benefits." Washington, D.C.: Institute for International Economics. Photocopy.

Rodriguez, F., and D. Rodrik. 2001. "Trade Policy and Economic Growth: A Skeptic's Guide to Cross-National Evidence." In Ben S. Bernanke and Kenneth Rogoff, eds., *Macroeconomics Annual 2000*. Cambridge, Mass.: National Bureau of Economic Research.

Rodrik, Dani. 1994. "The Rush to Free Trade in the Developing World: Why So Late? Why Now? Will It Last?" In S. Haggard and S. Webb, eds., *Voting for Reform: Democracy, Political Liberalization, and Economic Adjustment.* New York, N.Y.: Oxford University Press.

Rodrik, D. 1998. *Has Globalization Gone Too Far?* Washington, D.C.: Institute for International Economics.

Rogoff, Kenneth. 2005. "Paul Samuelson's Contributions to International Economics." Unpublished chapter intended for volume in honor of Paul Samuelson's 90th birthday.

Rubin, Robert E., and Jacob Weisberg. 2003. *In an Uncertain World: Tough Choices From Wall Street to Washington.* New York, N.Y.: Random House.

Ruhl, K.J. 2003. "Solving the elasticity puzzle in international economics." Unpublished.

Sachs, J.D., and H. Shatz. 1994. Trade and jobs in U.S. manufacturing. *Brookings Papers on Economic Activity.* Vol. 1, pp. 1-84.

Scheve, Kenneth, and Matthew Slaughter. 2007. A new deal for globalization. *Foreign Affairs.* Vol. 86, No. 4.

Schmitt, J., and L. Mishel. 1996. "Did international trade lower less-skilled wages during the 1980s? Standard theory and evidence." Technical Paper. Washington, D.C.: Economic Policy Institute.

Schumer, C., and P.C. Roberts. 2004. Second thoughts on free trade. *New York Times,* January 6.

Senses, Mine. 2006. "The effects of outsourcing on the elasticity of labor demand." Working Paper. Washington, D.C.: Johns Hopkins University School of Advanced International Studies

Slaughter, M.J. 2000. "What Are the Results of Product Price Studies and What Can We Learn From Their Differences?" In R.C. Feenstra, ed., *International Trade and Wages.* University of Chicago Press and the National Bureau of Economic Research.

Slaughter, M.J. 2001. International trade and labor: demand elasticities. *Journal of International Economics.* Vol. 54, No. 1, pp. 27-56.

Thierfelder, K., and S. Robinson. 1996. "The trade-wage debate in a model with nontraded goods: Making room for labor economists in trade theory." Discussion Paper No. 9. Washington, D.C.: International Food Policy Research Institute, Trade and Macroeconomics Division.

Tang, P., and A. Wood. 1997. "Globalization, co-operation costs, and wage inequalities." Working Paper, University of Sussex.

Trefler, D. 1995. The case of the missing trade and other mysteries. *American Economic Review.* Vol. 85, No. 1, pp. 1029-46.

Trefler, D., and S. Zhu. 2005. "The structure of factor content predictions." Working Paper No. 11221. Cambridge, Mass.: National Bureau of Economic Research.

Van Welsum, D., and G. Vickery. 2005. "New perspectives on ICT skills and employment." Information Economy Working Paper. Paris: Organization for Economic Cooperation and Development.

Verhoogen, Eric. 2004. "Trade, quality upgrading, and wage inequality in the Mexican manufacturing sector." Working Paper, University of California-Berkeley Center for Labor Economics. Berkeley, Calif.: Center for Labor Economics.

Wood, A. 1994. *North-South Trade, Employment, and Inequality.* Oxford: Clarendon Press.

Wood, A. 1995. How trade hurt unskilled workers. *Journal of Economic Perspectives.* Vol. 9, No. 3, pp. 57-80.

World Bank. 2002. *Global Economic Prospects and the Developing Countries 2002.* Washington, D.C.: World Bank.

About EPI

THE ECONOMIC POLICY INSTITUTE was founded in 1986 to widen the debate about policies to achieve healthy economic growth, prosperity, and opportunity. Today, despite rapid growth in the U.S. economy in the latter part of the 1990s, inequality in wealth, wages, and income remains historically high. Expanding global competition, changes in the nature of work, and rapid technological advances are altering economic reality. Yet many of our policies, attitudes, and institutions are based on assumptions that no longer reflect real world conditions.

With the support of leaders from labor, business, and the foundation world, the Institute has sponsored research and public discussion of a wide variety of topics: globalization; fiscal policy; trends in wages, incomes, and prices; education; the causes of the productivity slowdown; labor market problems; rural and urban policies; inflation; state-level economic development strategies; comparative international economic performance; and studies of the overall health of the U.S. manufacturing sector and of specific key industries.

The Institute works with a growing network of innovative economists and other social-science researchers in universities and research centers all over the country who are willing to go beyond the conventional wisdom in considering strategies for public policy. Founding scholars of the Institute include Jeff Faux, former EPI president; Lester Thurow, Sloan School of Management, MIT; Ray Marshall, former U.S. secretary of labor, professor at the LBJ School of Public Affairs, University of Texas; Barry Bluestone, Northeastern University; Robert Reich, former U.S. secretary of labor; and Robert Kuttner, author, editor of *The American Prospect*, and columnist for *Business Week* and the *Washington Post* Writers Group.

For additional information about the Institute, contact EPI at 1333 H St. NW, Suite 300, Washington, DC 20005, (202) 775-8810, or visit www.epi.org.

OTHER BOOKS FROM
THE ECONOMIC POLICY INSTITUTE

The State of Working America 2008/2009
by Lawrence Mishel, Jared Bernstein,
and Heidi Shierholz

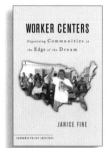

Worker Centers
Organizing Communities at the Edge of the Dream
by Janice Fine

Good Jobs, Bad Jobs, No Jobs
Labor Markets and Informal Work in Egypt,
El Salvador, India, Russia, and South Africa
byTony Avirgan, L. Josh Bivens &
Sarah Gammage, eds.

Talking Past Each Other
by David Kusnet, Lawrence Mishel,
Ruy Teixeira

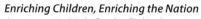

Enriching Children, Enriching the Nation
Public Investment in High-Quality Prekindergarten
by Robert G. Lynch

The Teaching Penalty
Teacher Pay Losing Ground
by Sylvia Allegretto, Sean P. Corcoran,
and Lawrence Mishel

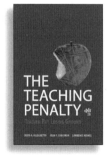

Order these and other EPI books at **www.epi.org**